Mind your own business!

by Murray Raphel

edited by Neil Raphel

Published by:
Raphel Marketing

Cover design by: Donna Huyett/Studio 151

Manufactured in the United States of America

ISBN 0-9624808-0-0

Library of Congress Catalog Card Number 89-092386

To Shirley and Milton Gordon,

We mind our business together.

MURRAY RAPHEL

TABLE OF CONTENTS

PART TWO
TARGETING YOUR CUSTOMER

FOREWORD

One of my favorite Murray Raphel stories concerns a supermarket near his home. The store's management, seeking to promote their friendly cashiers, ran a series of advertisements saying: "If one of our cashier ever forget to say 'Thank you, have a nice day,' we will give you one dollar."

A few weeks went by. One. day, Murray and his wife Ruth stopped at the store to see if its people were living up to the ad's promise. They shopped for a few items and arrived at the checkout counter. After taking their money, the cashier handed over the change — minus the friendly greeting.

"Aha!" Murray said. "You owe us a dollar."

"Why?" asked the bewildered cashier.

Murray, smiling, patiently explained the terms of the ad. The cashier smiled back. "I don't have to give you a dollar," she said, "That was last month's campaign."

We chuckle at the story. Yet we all know of businesses where we might expect the same reaction — where treating the customer well is considered a temporary phenomenon. Here, in "Mind Your Own Business," we find the opposite philosophy. Simply stated, it's: "Find out what your customers want and then give it to them." If you do it again and again, you'll never have to worry about sales or profit. Murray Raphel believes that there is one basic ingredient that all successful businesses have in common . . . "They take good care of their customers."

For years, I've been learning from Murray Raphel through his keynote addresses at the Food Marketing Institute Conventions. Crowds are always "standing room only." Thousands of others have heard him preach his beliefs worldwide, from Australia and the Far East to Europe and the United States. Murray Raphel knows what he's talking about.

We've all read books and heard speeches by experts advising us on customer service. Murray Raphel adds something more. He actually owns his own business! It's a successful multi-million dollar shopping complex called "Gordon's Alley" in Atlantic City, New Jersey. Murray has also been chosen New Jersey Retailer of the Year!

Murray knows what it's like to meet a payroll every week. He also knows what it feels like to bask in the glow of his own happy customers. Advice from such a man is priceless. You can count on it! He's put it to the test in his own laboratory.

This book could be called "The Best of Murray Raphel." It's chock-full of such gold nuggets as:

... Few customers do business with the Chairman of the Board. The customers reaction to your store is determined by how they are greeted and treated by each and every individual.

... Hire a couple of nicely dressed high school youths and have them take a survey. Ask customers what they like and don't like about your store. The results may be different from what you expect.

... Create an individual identity for your advertisement so that even it you leave your name off your ads, readers will recognize that it's you.

In addition, these pages are also sprinkled with some of the best oriental wisdom. From the Chinese proverb, "He who cannot smile should not own a shop" to the Japanese word for customer. . . "O-Kyaku-San." It means, "visitor to one's home." They're each superb reminders that there are few brand new ideas in this world. . . As the adage states, "everything has been thought of before; the problem is to think of it again."

So if you've been searching for a special book with the secrets of business success all in one spot, your search is over. "Mind Your Own Business" is for you. You may want to devour its pages all at one sitting. Or you may want to savor it, one chapter at a time like I did. Whatever your preference, I urge you to pick up your yellow highlighter and get started. My own advance copy of the manuscript now has so many of my yellow highlights that you'd think it was printed on yellow paper. I predict that Murray Raphel will be of great benefit to you — just as he has been to me.

Stew Leonard
Norwalk, CT
September, 1989

(Stew Leonard is the owner of **Stew Leonard's,** one of the most successful supermarket operations in the United States.)

INTRODUCTION

First of all, I'm a businessman.

That's how I think of myself.

That's how I want to be introduced when I give a speech.

And that's why I wanted to write this book. For the past 40 years I have owned, operated, advertised for, worried over and cared for a shopping complex we call Gordon's Alley in Atlantic City, New Jersey.

When I'm on the road to give a speech, I call our store every day just to make sure everything's all right.

I have meetings about our store at night.

Sometimes I wake up early in the morning thinking about our store.

Having a store is like having a baby.
* *

Many of the articles in the book originally appeared in **Direct Marketing** magazine and are included through the courtesy of my friend and early mentor, Pete Hoke, founder of **Direct Marketing** magazine. That's why you will read a lot about Direct Mail in this book. And, if you're not sure what Direct Mail is and how it works, I like the definition former U. S. Postmaster General William F. Bolger wrote in his introduction to **"The Do-It-Yourself Direct Mail Handbook"** that I wrote with Ken Erdman:

"Direct Mail is basically a sales message delivered by mail.

It's a person-to-person, company-to-company, highly identified medium that can pinpoint its audience, personalize its message and measure the results through orders or inquiries returned to the sender. A medium that is truly the message."

But when I re-read the articles, I realize the themes touched upon ideas that are broader than Direct Mail.

In fact, the chapters are divided rather evenly into three sections: Retail Operations, Direct Mail and Selling. And the audience for ALL these articles are people like myself: owners and operators of small businesses.

There are rules, guidelines, examples, stories and exhortations. All of the chapters are related to the basic concept of the book: By minding (and mining) your own business, you can increase your sales. And make your customers happy.
* *

For many years, we lived in an apartment located directly on top of our store.

During the day we would wait on customers.

At dinnertime, we would discuss how we handled our customers, what they bought and how we would increase our customer base the following day, week, year.

And, sometimes after dinner, we would return back into the store, to straighten the merchandise, get caught up on paperwork or redo our in-store displays.

Our other children would understand.

They would play in the store, pretending to wait on customers and helping us put away merchandise.

Our store was, is and will be an important family member.

Part One

Managing Your Business

I'd Like You To Meet My Best Friend

People constantly get us mixed up although our physical characteristics differ widely.

I was around at the birth and watched the growth. I suffered with the defeats and rejoiced in the triumph. I saw the physical changes through the years and watched maturity settle in. I've seen the expansion in size and structure and respect in the community.

Because of our closeness, others ask me to make decisions for my friend because they believe we think exactly alike. That's understandable. They see the two of us together for so many hours each day, some wonder if we are really one and the same person.

We are not. We each have our own identity. And though many of our thoughts, ideas, directions, and plans are similar, we each have our own individual personalities. I sometimes find the things I hesitate to do my friend does quickly. And vice-versa.

I sometimes envy, occasionally resent, but always respect his presence. Others have accused me of being overprotective and say, "Nothing will happen if you go away for a week or so." I have gone away and everything did work.

But, when I come back and find him there waiting, I am happy and content and eager to join in another adventure next week, next month, next year.

My friend, you see, is my business.

Through the years, those in the community find it difficult to understand that a business and an owner can really be two different personalities.

How does this "personality" come about? And how do you communicate your store's individuality to your customers?

Think about it for a minute. If someone asks you to describe a store in your town, you would use the same adjectives to describe a neighbor: "Kind, courteous, friendly, cares about people." Or, "Nasty, mean, makes you wait. I hate being there. . ."

Think about restaurants where you have dined. Some you cannot wait to bring friends to, to share the experience. Other places you advise friends not to go for many reasons. Near the top of the "reasons why" list is the attitude the "restaurant has." (Note: Not the owner, but the restaurant.)

Successful retailers tell you they can walk into a store and immediately "feel" if it's successful. There need not be crowds of people. There is a mysterious omnipresent aura that seeps into the psyche and one knows, feels, understands whether or not the store is happy, content. . . successful.

Successful retailers understand this philosophy and work toward developing the personality of their store. They create an ambiance that is warm, comfortable and makes people want to come back again. And again. And again. And again. And. . . .

One way is to make sure the people who work in your business understand this sensitive, invisible, difficult-to-explain "feeling" that becomes a part of the environment when customers call or arrive.

Ted Cohn, well-known lecturer from New Jersey, once addressed a group of supermarket owners and asked one, "How many people work in your store?" The man answered, "I have about 80 people working for me."

"Really?" said Ted, "If you have about 80 people working for you, most will leave by the end of the year."

The retailer was shocked, and insisted Ted explain. He did.

"You see," he said "when people work **for** you they are no longer individuals. They are employees. They simply cannot become excited about your business. But if your statement was 'I have 80 people who work **with** me,' then this feeling would be reflected in your business. Customers would sense it, and most of your personnel will still be with you in the years to come."

His point: Few people do business with the chairman of the board of the bank, the owner of the supermarket or the man or woman who started a retail store. The customer's reaction to your business —and your business' personality—is determined by how they are greeted and treated by each and every one of the individuals working in your business. Working, hopefully, "with" you.

Each should feel if he or she were not able to show up for work in the morning because of sickness or an emergency, you would have grave doubts about starting the day. You make each one feel your business is a composite of all of them and functions at its peak performance only when they are all there to contribute to the the total image.

What about the "look" your business gives to customers before they call or come in for products or services?

Think about your direct mail. Ed Mayer, one of the original direct marketing experts, suggests several cardinal direct mail rules: One is, "Make the layout and copy fit." Certainly a men's clothing store should not send out mailers in a feminine script on pink scented paper. And a women's specialty shop will not use heavy Barnum lettering on thick rough paper.

Your mailer should be recognized as your store.

We once forgot to put our store's name on the outside envelope. It was mentioned only once in the inside copy. We asked customers how they knew the mailer they received was from us. "It looked like your store," they said.

We are proud, possessive and positively passionate about maintaining out business' individual identity. We think about new promotions, toss ideas around for advertising and mailing pieces and often one of us says, "No, it doesn't look like our business." Translation: It is not what people expect of our retail operation. We find to our delight and sometimes to our frustration that the business is expected to act, perform, participate (or not participate) in a certain manner.

You may wonder if your perception of your business' image is the same as your customer's.

Here's one way to find out. Hire a couple of nicely dressed high school students. Have them do random research with your customers. Put together a handful of questions including, "What do you like best (and least) about shopping in this store?" Give them a quick checklist of descriptive adjectives for customers to pick and choose in identifying your store. Make the range wide enough to include the obvious contrasts ("friendly-unfriendly") and special services ("free delivery," "easy refunds," "guarantees").

When you tabulate the answers you will see the community has put together an image of your stores that may be somewhat different than you think it is. Study the results. As Johnny Mercer once wrote, you can then begin to "Acc-en-tuate the Positive and e-li-min-ate the Negative." And the customer will refuse to buy the merchandise from your store unless it has your label sewn in and your name on top of the box.

I bring this to your attention because my friend just celebrated his 40th birthday. And though I'm 20 years older than my business, people say we think alike, share the same philosophy and are inseparable. Almost. But not quite.

2 Ten Rules For Writing A Good Headline

1. Self Interest.
What benefit does the headline offer the reader? One of the best selling headlines of all times, Dale Carnegie's "How To Win Friends and Influence People" was the **third** title he tried.

It worked because everyone wants to have friends. And influence people.

Other self interest headlines that work:

"How to lose 10 pounds in 10 days."

"How to retire on $25,000 a year."

"Are you spending $10.00 a week too much for food?"

2. Arouse Curiosity.
Stop your reader with a statement that makes them ask, "How can that be?" And/or, "What do they mean by that?"

Examples:

"Do you wonder how we can sell an all wool shetland sweater for less than $15.00?"

"How to look younger in 14 days."

"How many of these 20 questions can you answer correctly?"

Important: You must **answer** the question you raise in the headline in the copy that follows. And the answer must make logical sense. Because you make a special purchase. Because you are offering your customers a pre-season chance to buy before you advertise to the world. The customer's curiosity must be satisfied by your explanation. Otherwise they will simply not respond and, more important, have grave skepticism about future mailings from you.

A shocking statistic we recently read: 90 percent of Americans do NOT associate the word "trust" with the word "business."

And "trust" is a key word in your business.

3. The Right Audience.
Whom do you want to read your ad? Does your headline single them out?

The two most important ingredients in a successful direct mail package are (1) the List and (2) the Offer.

You start off with a giant advantage, the List. Your own customers. People who trust and believe you because they have invested their money with you in the past.

Your customers are obviously your right audience. When looking to expand your mailing list by using new lists, make sure these names are as close as possible to your present customers in terms of age/salary/where they live and how they live.

The Offer means you do not offer a product the customer does NOT want. Too much waste of time and money.

Some of the direct mail experts say the best mailer is only 20 percent devoted to creativity. The other 80 percent is divided equally between the right offer. . . and the right list.

4. Make It Easy To Understand.
Most of us talk two languages. One when we are talking to one another. The second when we sit down to write something. We suddenly become a different person, very erudite and much more difficult to understand. When writing a headline (or copy), make it **easy** to understand.

And do NOT talk in terms of the features of the product. But talk of benefits. Forget the detailed analysis. Say what the item will do for the reader.

What does **that** mean?

If the jacket is down-filled say, "Twice the warmth at half the weight."

If an insurance policy has lower rates for non-smokers say, "Double the coverage for the same premium."

5. Make It Newsworthy.

Look at the direct mail pieces you receive in the mail. Notice how many times you see these words in headlines of newspaper ads: New. Announcing. For the first time. Introducing.

There's a reason. They work.

Cereals and soups are constantly promoted as "new and improved."

Customers respond favorably to that which is new, the latest, just out. Everyone wants to be at the front of the line when the store opens.

6. Make it Believable.

The headline that begins, "This is your last chance to . . . " is the one I never finish reading. I know a similar (or better) offer will follow in the next mail.

We agree with David Ogilvy's line, "The customer is not a moron. She's your wife."

Writers who look for the cute (and irrelevant) phrase, the clever pun, the gimmick, wind up with headlines that are often looked at . . . but not believed.

If you offer a well known product at too low a price the customer asks themselves, "What's the gimmick, angle, reason? It simply does not make sense." It is not believable. And therefore ignored.

7. Quick Results.

Americans are accustomed to speed. The success of the newspaper *USA Today* is because it closely parallels the nightly TV news. A condensation of what happened that day without too much information. Everything is complete on one page. And preferably in one or two paragraphs.

If you can show how someone can lose weight quickly, make money quickly, be successful in a short period of time, people will read what you have to say.

8. Be Specific.
What does a "half price sale" mean?

Yes, it means one half the original price. But if you do not say the original price. . . uh, what does "half price sale" mean?

When banks offer savings in terms of percentages. . . what do the percentages mean? If they would offer the return in terms of dollars. . . well, that we understand.

People have a strange attraction to numbers. From the Ten Commandments to the "Seven out of 10 people who. . . " to the "19 reasons why" to the "16 people who believe that . . ." Not only do people read the headline and then start reading the copy. . . but, more amazingly, they feel they have to read down to the last number mentioned.

The more specific you are in your headline, the more selective you are in choosing your audience. Examples:

"An important message to men who are losing their hair. . . "
"How college students can earn their tuition this summer. . . "

9. Something of Value.
The cosmetics people have this down to an exact science. They call it "purchase with purchase." If you buy one of their products, you receive a gift for free or for a fraction of its true value.

Offer benefits you have that make you separate, different and (hopefully) in front of the competition: free parking, free gift wrapping, free delivery, free monogramming. . .

10. Make It Well Known.
David Ogilvy said, "Include the brand name in the headline." A good idea. Whenever possible. Putting in the name just for putting in the name is not good enough.

If your name has a **reason** for being there, fine. Because you are the first to . . . because you are the place where. . . because you are known for. . . all good reasons. But simply putting your store's name **without a reason** may make **you** feel good but will not do a thing for your customer.

Brand names are important because they make the reader feel comfortable. They know about a specific brand and will respond in a more positive manner than an unfamiliar brand.

Use testimonials. Customers react positively to endorsements by well-known people. (Otherwise why are all these advertising agencies paying all that money?) Many sport celebrities earn much more on the testimonial circuit than on the playing field.

Reason why: They are well known.

Next time you write a headline for your business, check what-you-wrote against the ten rules above. If the words do not fit one of the categories above, try, try again. It was David Ogilvy who had his new copywriters come up with 100 different headlines for each ad.

3 The Day We Gave A Parade And Nobody Came

"Let me tell you about the advertising campaign I did that bombed. . . " When was the last time you heard someone start a conversation with THAT sentence?

All we read about in magazines and textbooks and classroom studies are winners.

Aren't there any losers? Yes.

Can we gain anything by reading about them? Yes.

Does anybody write about them? No.

Here's why: One day, I thought it would be a great idea to write a book about direct mail campaigns that flopped. And why. What a marvelous opportunity to prove to everyone even the experts don't do it right EVERY time. I wrote friends in the business for their most tragic story and promised if they told me theirs, I'd tell them mine and and we'd put them all in a book.

A book? For strangers to read and know they had failed? Even one time! Uh. . . thanks, but no thanks.

They wrote back saying, "My client won't let me". . . "I don't have the information anymore because I've blocked it out of my memory. . ." "Can I tell you about a recent success instead?" And so it went.

With one exception: John Fraser Robinson, "Mr. Direct Mail," of England.

John has won (and continues to win) prizes in direct mail in the U.K. and Europe. Some of his returns on mailings far exceed the most optimistic projections. He is an international speaker on direct mail and wrote the chapter on creativity in the official U.K. Post Office Direct Mail Handbook. His newest book, "The Secrets Of Effective Direct Mail," is an easy-to-read-and-follow guide for . . . effective direct mail.

First his mistakes. Then ours.

He still remembers the ones he can laugh about (Only gently. It still hurts). Among the sad memories. . .

"The promotion for the electric typewriter where the mailing forgot to say it was electric. Everyone thought it was the most expensive manual typewriter they ever saw. . . "

"And then there was the time I talked an old schoolmate into switching his business over to mail order. He put his first job into the mail so late, the season was over and no one wanted his product."

"Which was topped by a job lot of 400 hair products I bought in the mid-60s. I produced the campaign copy and design, selected and booked the media, ran it and waited for the mail and the checks. Out of 400, I sold seven. Four were returned for refunds."

"But the best was how I earned my first job: by mail. Very scientific. I selected three companies. Sent them each three mailings. But I didn't do my homework and the three companies were all in the same group. I was interviewed by a man with all nine letters on his desk. He loved it. He made me a van driver."

I sympathized with John but said no one equalled the day we gave a parade and nobody came.

The time was St. Patrick's Day, 1975.

I had become enthused with the Neiman-Marcus Fortnight promotions in Dallas, Texas. Two solid weeks of selling merchandise from India. Or China. Or Ireland. Or Israel. Or some place other than home.

If it worked for Stanley Marcus, why wouldn't it work for me? We had just returned from our first overseas trip to Ireland. "Let's put on an Irish fortnight show!" we said. "We'll give away a ticket on Aer Lingus. We will promote made-in-Ireland merchandise including sweaters, china and food."

And to make sure it will be a tremendous success, we'll kick it off on St. Patrick's Day. How could we miss?

Since promotions work best when you keep coming up with ideas, we kept coming up with ideas.

For Monday, St. Patrick's Day, we would welcome the Irish consul to town! But the Irish consul is asked to appear in dozens of cities throughout the United States on St. Patrick's Day. Undaunted, we went to the consul's New York City Office with a letter from our mayor asking him to come to Atlantic City. Impressed, they gave me the vice consul for the day.

But the piece de resistance was our big climax: **We would have Atlantic City's first St. Patrick's Day parade at the end of the promotion!**

Next: We contacted a local set designer and arranged for him to design "thatched roofs" for the fronts of our store. Boy, were we authentic!

A visit to Aer Lingus followed. We told them the story of the parade (did you see the letter from our mayor?), and told them that the Irish deputy consul, Padraic O'Coileain himself, would be there. We renamed our shopping center O'Gordon's Alley for the two-week period. Now, could we please have two free tickets to Ireland?

They were so excited they offered to send down staff people for the parade and the drawing for the tickets.

And then we sent out our mailer!

It was in the shape of an Irish shamrock. When you opened it up, you saw the events we had in store for you for the next 14 days (fortnight).

The first day was fine. Padraic O'Coileain, the deputy consul general of Ireland, came to a flag-rising ceremony at City Hall and flew the Irish flag beside the American.

He dined on Irish stew at our restaurant and customers came in to see him, say hello and buy merchandise.

So far, so good.

The second day we offered another "special Irish luncheon."

The third day we had an original Irish musical in the store performed by local five-year-olds.

By the fourth day, we were recommending customers visit OTHER local Irish restaurants.

On the fifth day, we reminded them to come see our Irish "thatched roof" cottages. (But hadn't they seen that the first day?)

But Saturday, ah Saturday, that was the day of the parade!

We hired a Mummer's Band to come in from Philadelphia.

Now, to the unaware reader, a Mummer's Band plays in the Mummer's parade (naturally) held every New Year's Day in Philadelphia. Mummers belong to clubs and rehearse all year long for this all-day parade.

Their costumes are feathered, jeweled and gaudy, and they play saxophones, banjos and glockenspiels.

We hired a band to come down on their bus to march in the first St. Patrick's Day parade in our town. And we would march up front with the leader!

They came, they rehearsed, they marched. And we led the parade!

But no one came to see us.

A few car horns beeped appreciatively. Some late going-to-work pedestrians wondered what the noise was all about. We banjoed and saxaphoned and glockenspieled down the city's main street for 20 blocks to the waiting bus. The Mummers piled in and headed back to Philadephia with the last one asking, "Was that a dress rehearsal? Where were the people?"

When looking back later on what went wrong, we concluded it was just TOO long a promotion. One day, great; two days, maybe. Two weeks: Never.

Now our promotions last a day. And the better ones last a few hours.

But we'll always remember the day we gave a parade and nobody came. If only it had rained on our parade. At least we could have cancelled.

4

The Five Ways Advertising Works

The patient wakes up in the hospital room after the operation. She looks around and asks, "**Where** am I?"

She does not ask, "**How** am I?" which you might think would be the normal reaction. "Not so," say doctors. The first words are directed to being in a **familiar** situation.

This basic need is one of the five ways advertising works.

Question: Are there rules, concepts, guidelines we can use in our advertising to make sure it works all the time?

Answer: No. John Wanamaker knew that at the turn of the century when he said "Half the money I spend on advertising is wasted. I only wish I knew which half."

BUT... there are certain rules that seem to work **MOST** of the time. Five of them were pointed out more than 20 years ago by James Webb Young, a director of J. Walter Thompson and recognized by many as the dean of American advertising. He said if you want to succeed in advertising, you have to remember there are only five ways advertising works. Your job: Check your advertising to see if it meets one (or more) of these five rules.

Here they are:

1. Be familiar.
2. Be a reminder.
3. Be newsworthy.

4. Be action-stimulating.

5. Be able to add value to the product.

Let's look at them one-by-one and see how they work for you:

1. People want to be in a familiar setting (our example in the first paragraph). And/or buy a familiar product. Once buying habit patterns are set, they are difficult to change.

Friends like to take you to a restaurant **they** enjoyed, buy a car **they** appreciate, purchase a book **they** have read.

Ever drive down an unfamiliar road at nighttime? Notice how much longer the drive seems than in. . . daytime? Reason: It is simply not "familiar" to you.

When you go shopping you reach for the brands you are "familiar" with — either because you used them before, or because you have seen the name over and over again in advertising. That is the reason no-name generic food advertising makes up only a tiny fraction of the food business. The saving in dollars is not strong enough to overcome the lack of recognition.

This is also the reason you see advertising which hammers the name of the product over and over in the commercial. The advertiser wants to implant the name in your subconscious so when you see it in the marketplace you will respond with, "Oh, yes, that name IS familiar to me. . . "

Psychologists call this the "degree of comfort." You do not have to make a decision on whether or not the purchase will serve your needs. It did before. It will again. You are certainly comfortable making the decision to buy.

What does that have to do with your mailing to your customer?

This: **You passed the first test.** Because your customer IS familiar with you. And is the reason they will open up AND READ what you have mailed them.

A recent readership survey revealed that people who owned or had purchased a product were twice as apt to read an advertisement of the product than someone who had never bought the product

Familiarity. It works. To bring the customer in.

2. Look at the calender. Every month has several holidays. Most are put there as a reason for buying. Valentine's Day. Halloween. Christmas. Mother's and Father's and Grandmother's and Grandfather's Day. Industries lobby for the mayor or governor or President to proclaim a "day" for their individual industry.

Reason: To encourage people to buy that product. To call attention to and start a habit pattern for the sale of that particular product or service. And once you set a habit pattern, it is difficult to stop. Think about it: Fish on Fridays. Hot cross buns for Easter.

The raisin industry wanted to increase sales of their product so they promoted, "Fresh raisin bread on Wednesday." It worked.

Summer business is slow on Saturday. Our store ran a series of specials for this one day only and promoted the slogan, "If it's Saturday, it must be Gordon's Alley." (Reminding!)

Our largest single business day is on New Year's Day. We promote this opening day of our fall and winter sale ONLY by direct mail. No radio. No newspaper. No TV. Nothing except direct mail. People know when it will happen and have appeared regularly **for the past 25 years!** All we do is remind them.

And how about political parties? A few weeks before the election you are **reminded** to vote and HOW to vote.

And your church sends you a bulletin to tell you what is happening at services this week, **reminding** you.

Shoe stores send out notes every few months to tell you it is time to come in for a new pair of shoes for your children's growing feet.

Joe Girard (America's #1 salesman) spends more than $25,000 a year just on post cards to his customers. One every month. To **remind** them of the holiday that month and also that he is still around selling the same merchandise in the same place at the same address. Reminding.

And then there's Ben Feldman from East Liverpool, Ohio, selling insurance for New York Life and America's number one salesman. One technique he uses: A letter to his customers who have a birthday coming up. He attaches a crisp, new $1 bill to the note telling them their premium will go up **$1 a day after** their birthday and they should be thinking of buying **before** that time arrives.

Results: More than $7 million written every year by just this simple technique.

Reminding: It works. To bring the customer back.

3. Public relations people make their money by being newsworthy. Can they come up with something that would make the news column instead of the advertising columns?

There was a time when the first signs of fall were the shedding of leaves, the cool nip of night air and the introduction of the new model cars. That was news! And people came to see, admire and buy.

The arrival of the personal computer was news. And each subsequent addition, edition and improvement was news. And sells computers.

Notice how many times you see the word "new" atop soap powder and cereals. Because "New" IS "news."

(CAUTION: Just because it IS new and news does NOT mean it will sell. Only a tiny percentage of "new" products introduced every year succeed. For the product or service must not only be new — but must also supply a need or be an improvement over a comparable product already on the market.)

Opening a new department in your store?

Creating early opening or late opening hours?

Running a special promotion and/or sale you want your regular customers to know about before anyone else?

Newsworthy. It works. To bring the customers reasons to buy.

4. Advertising expert James Webb Young tells of the time he ran a mail order color-page in **Life** magazine. The page received a Starch "read most" rating of 20 percent. But, the response in orders was only 1/10th of one percent of the circulation.

What happened? People read the ad. But only a small percentage "acted" on the ad. The bottom line of good advertising is not how many awards are won at annual ceremonies, but how much money is put in the register. Salesmen know this. The "close" of the sale is the most important part.

It is fine to have a marvelous introduction. It is commendable to have a package of reasons why people should buy. But they both mean nothing if no sale takes place. Salesmen are taught to remember the ABC's of selling: Always Be Closing. They are reminded by their sales managers over and over again to AFTO— Ask For The Order.

Direct response people agree. They tell you to ask for the order within the ad, on the order blank, on the envelope. The customers must be told what they have to do in order to buy, purchase and receive the merchandise. The average newspaper has less than 100 editorial stories and two to three times as many ads. How do we motivate readers to the point where they pick up a pencil and fill in their name, address, and credit card number?

The desire to act are already there down deep inside the consumer:

Everyone wants to have money for retirement. (So how do we have them start their Individual Retirement Account in our bank? Our insurance company? Our stock brokerage?)

Everyone wants to make sure their family is taken care of when they die. (So how do we have them buy our insurance?)

Everyone has to buy food and clothing. (So how do we have them come to our food store? Our clothing store?)

How do we overcome this inertia on the part of the customer? Listing impressive numbers are ho-hum. We must use a carrot and/or a stick — a reward or punishment, in words or pictures, or both.

Sometimes words alone will help. Life insurance is not sold in England or Australia, but life assurance is. That has a different sound. If insurance means they pay off when I leave, does assurance mean I'm going to be around a while longer?

Ask yourself: "What am I doing today to sell the merchandise I have?" A speaker once went around the room with people from different businesses. He asked each of them, "What are you going to do tomorrow?"

The real estate agent said he was going to show some houses. The insurance salesperson said he was going to line up some physicals for customers. The clothing salesperson said he was going to show some clothes. But not one said, "I'm going to make a sale."

Making the appeal to a specific audience will always result in a higher return. National magazines become extinct, but new magazines spring up weekly for specific groups. (Count the number of computer magazines on your newsstand today.)

Action stimulating. It works to make the customer buy.

5. See those boxes of baking soda in refrigerators all over America making them smell nicer! But, isn't baking soda supposed to be used for baking?

Sure. But the company came up with *another and additional* reason to buy the product. They practiced line extension. If you own a major share of the market with what you make, how can you add *new* market?

Shake'n Bake advertises the product as a base for a pie as well as a coating for chicken.

L'eggs mails a catalog to nurses offering only white panty hose.

Hershey chocolate finds a winner when it markets chocolate milk in a candy bar look-alike container.

Gerber baby food adds its name and reputation to baby clothing and accessories.

Prestige can also be "added value." The Polo horse on your shirt; the "CM" for Countess Mara on your tie; the package from Tiffany's for the wedding present; the Avanti car; the Movado watch; the Steuben glass, the Rosenthal China.

Added value. It works. It gives an "extra" reason why the customer should buy.

Add all five of these Reasons Why Advertising Works together and you have a powerful chance for success.

5 Stealing the Competition

There is an island called Ulawa in the Eastern Solomon Islands. The natives who live there believe you can frighten trees to death by simply yelling at them. If there is a tree too big to be chopped down, you can kill it by creeping up on it very early in the morning and suddenly letting loose with a piercing scream. Now the tree doesn't fall right away. You have to keep yelling at the tree every morning for a month or more. They believe the tree finally goes into shock and dies from being yelled at so violently and so often. Now some trees do fall and do die-- from old age and from winds. But the Ulawans are convinced the trees fell because they yelled and screamed at them. And no one has been able to convince them otherwise.

In the fight to find new customers, businesses are starting to use a heretofore sacrosanct and untouched opportunity: The OTHER GUY'S customer. They yell out their name and try Ulawa-fashion to scare them to death. What this means: If I can't attract enough new people to buy/try my product, I'll take your customers away from you! Despite David Ogilvy's warning to never mention the competition, much of today's businesses do just that. They believe if they yell at the competition long and loud enough, they will fall down and die just like the trees on Ulawa.

There are two reason for this marketing switch:

1. There are too many stores.

Every time a new business opens, it takes a piece from an existing business. For many years economists said, "That doesn't hurt anyone because the business pie keeps on getting bigger and so you can take out more pieces." No more. The pie is getting smaller. Or at least staying the same. It is no longer enough to simply say how-good-we-are but rather how-much-better-we-are-than-all-others.

2. The increased access to databases.

Direct mail and telephone marketing can isolate customers who shop one store or buy one product and offer them incentives to switch to the competition because, (A) There is no stronger believer than the converted believer and, (B) Once you have a customer switch and then shop your business four times in a row they develop a pattern of shopping with you and will stay. Unless you give them a reason to leave.

Fighting for a larger market share, major companies have turned to telemarketing and direct marketing companies to steal customers form the competition. In the past this was done gently. A business simply said about their product, "Try it, you'll like it." This is not the case anymore. Today they not only tell you why their product is better — but also tell you why the competitive product is worse.

In the United States there are no prohibitions against naming the competition or even saying why you are better. The only watchdog is the advertising industry itself, which sets up guidelines to follow and has boards to judge complaints of unfair advertising. But even it they tell a company the advertising is untrue, the company does not have to change the advertising so judged. They can keep on running the ad. (Most do not for fear of bad press.)

In direct contrast, comparison advertising is against the law in Germany. You cannot mention the competitive product by name. You cannot give comparisons between your product and theirs. In most Scandinavian countries, comparisons **are** allowed. In France, where you cannot mention the competition, companies obliquely side-step the rule by crossing out what is obviously the competition's name in an advertisement. In Japan, comparative advertising is just starting. Here is a quote from Tadao Tanaka, legal head of Japan's ANA airlines: "As much as 10 percent of all Japanese advertising will be comparative in the near future." If Japan makes this statement, will other countries follow? The United States has not only started doing comparative ads, but it has hired direct marketing firms to have the customer decide they would rather switch than fight, to rephrase the old Marlboro campaign.

Here's how:

Couponing: Nearly 300 billion coupons were printed in the United States last year and distributed through mailboxes, freestanding inserts in newspaper and in run-of-the-paper ads. It is predicted that by 1990 there will be more than 350 billion coupons.

But only 4 percent are redeemed!

And even within this small percentage there is a lot of waste. Nearly nine out of 10 coupons are redeemed by customers currently using the same product! What's happening? The coupon people have violated a basic direct marketing rule: good offer, wrong list. This error is compounded even further when you realize many of the coupons go to people who cannot use them. Why offer dog food coupons to people who don't have dogs? Cigarette coupons to non-smokers? If only there was a way to find out who is using what product.

Aha — there is!

Catalina Marketing in California pinpoints the customer by installing special coupon printers at supermarkets that issue on-the-spot coupons. How does this technique work? Like this:

1. It eliminates coupons to those who don't need them. A machine at the check-out counter scans what the customer has bought, and then issues special coupons in the same categories. Now, dog food users receive dog food coupons.

2. It makes the customer switch next time they shop. If you bought Coca-Cola, the program can be designed to give you a coupon for money off on competitive Pepsi-Cola on your next shopping trip.

"Businesses are rewarding present customers and not attracting new customers," says Sam Gower, former chairman of Precision Target Marketing (PTM), whose firm came up with a better idea: Persuade the customer using one brand, store or product to switch to another brand, store or product.

PTM is not alone. Other businesses in the competition include Computerized Market Technology and John Blair Marketing. They send out questionaires in newspapers reaching 45 million U. S. households on a typical Sunday. Donnelley Marketing mails questionaires to 30 million households through its Carol Wright Direct Mail program.

PTM uses telemarketing. Their employees work at home calling five million customers just on the Eastern seaboard to ask, "What supermarket do you shop?" or "What product do you buy?" or "What car do you drive?" When they find out, PTM mails the consumer coupons from PTM's clients who are the **competitive** supermarket, product, car, etc. Its customer list includes Sears, Burger King, A & P supermarkets, Kraft cheese products, Lipton tea — even casinos in Atlantic City.

Here's how their program works:

In a five minute telephone interview, PTM's operator finds out where the customers are shopping, what they are shopping for and/or what they are buying.

Within three weeks the customers receive valuable coupons or samples persuading them to switch to PTM's client.

How is this direct marketing program working? Remember a few paragraphs back where only 4 percent of mailed-to-everyone coupons are redeemed? Compare that to a 15 percent to 30 percent redemption rate from the market pinpointed in the PTM program.

Does it work for every company? No. New products, new brands and names not well known do not have customer confidence and will not do as well. But when it works. . . it **really** works:

• Dorsey pharmacies (cough and cold remedies) was so impressed, it set aside 80 percent of its promotional budget for this telemarketing campaign.

• Genovese Drug stores saw its coupon redemption rate jump from 5 percent to 20 percent with this telemarketing program. More important: Their market share increased 53 percent simply by targeting people who were customers of their competition.

• When Stop & Shop supermarkets started the program, business jumped $30 million in just one year. "We were skeptical at first," said Arthur Patterson, the company's research manager. "I wondered, if it's so great, how come nobody else is doing it?"

Most of these companies follow PTM's suggestions for making the program really effective. When the special coupons are redeemed, the cashier **must** call the store manager or department head to come to the point of sale and personally thank the customer for shopping with them. Oh, by the way, did they like the store? Was everything OK? Did they receive the store's circular for that week? Are they on the store's mailing list? No? Hmmm. . . here's your application to fill out. Presto! Enlarged and enhanced database!

Sometimes the campaign can be carried to extremes. Consider the program of the First Bank & Trust Company of Harrisburg, Illinois. That bank decided it wanted to attract its competitor's customers, and so it offered new customers who switched to its bank a reward of . . . guns! Right, handguns. If you deposited $2,000 in a 10-year certificate of deposit, you were given a Smith and Wesson 9mm and .45 caliber automatic cartridge pistol valued at $1,200 — comparable to the amount of interest you would earn during the term of the certificate. (They dismissed the concerns of skeptics who wondered how the bank could be sure the money would remain for 10 years, since the customer now had a gun which could mean a much faster withdrawal.)

Question: Is there a defense for you, when attacked by the competitor?

Answer: Yes. And it is the same as the competition uses to attract **your** customers: direct marketing.

Although there may be a temporary jump in business when you attack the competition, the long-range benefits can be few. . . if any. Direct marketers should concentrate on doing what they do best to protect their existing database and also bring customers by stressing service and quality. It starts with remembering that direct response advertising is the most personal of all media. It is a one-on-one relationship with your customer that **no other** advertising can achieve.

A recent Gallup opinion poll of major U.S. companies asked the question: "What's the most important factor for your business to grow and succeed in the next three years?" The answer chosen by more than half: "service and quality." Proof of that was a study analyzing the performance of 2,600 businesses over the past 15 years. Results: "Businesses that offer high quality come out on top." Conclusion: "Customers will pay more for superior service." Case in point: Scandinavian Airlines went from steady losses to steady profits by concentrating on just their business travelers. They had this existing database in their computers. They put on earlier and later flights to accommodate this customer. They installed moveable partitions to expand their business class as needed. Said spokesperson Jan Carlson, "We coached staff to handle business travelers like royalty."

What do the leaders in direct marketing say? Here's a quote from Leon Gorman, president of L. L. Bean, one of America's most successful mail order companies: "Service is a day-in, day-out, ongoing, never-ending, unremitting, persevering, compassionate type of activity." OK. Fine. Terrific. If service is the answer to keeping customers from being stolen, are there rules to follow that work? Answer: Yes. (Well, most of the time.) There are five. Here they are:

1. **Hire the right people.**

Singapore Airlines employs less than 2 percent of the thousands of women who want to become "Singapore girls." They very carefully prescreen applicants to make sure their staff is customer-conscious. Here's why: A recent survey asked 700 major companies the question, "Does your salesman care about you and your business?" And 92 percent said, "No"!

One of the main things a business must do is **listen** to its customers. General Electric wanted to find out why its sales weren't increasing. It asked its customers the reason they were not doing more business. The most quoted answer: "Your salesmen talk too much." Direct marketers "listen" by TESTING. The number one rule in selling always has been to simply "Find out what the customer wants to buy. And give it to them." You can do that in direct response advertising by "listening" and "measuring results" and "testing."

2. Train them, motivate them, give them authority.

American Express gives cash awards up to $1,000 for great performers. Example: Barbara Weaver cut through miles of U. S. State Department red tape to refund $989 of stolen travelers' checks to a customer stranded in Cuba.

3. Invest early and heavily in technology to support customer service.

American Express plans to spend $300 million on technology to improve service. One year they followed-up 20,000 customer transactions to see how the customers rated the treatment they received. How important is this? THIS important: Most people do not complain. If they do complain and you answer the problem immediately, you not only keep the customer, you increase their sales with you and, MOST IMPORTANT, they become your best salespeople! They tell their neighbors, friends and business associates to hurry on down and buy YOUR product or service.

4. Keep an eye on the competition.

Simply yelling at the competition is not the best way. Yes, see what they are doing. Yes, watch them. But your goal is to have your competition keep an eye on YOU. What do YOU do that is innovative, different and unusual to enhance your database? **Simply show your customer you care about them as a customer.** Give them reasons to buy from you rather than from your competition.

One of the early moves in this direction was a Chrysler automobile ad in 1932, which was headlined, "Look At All Three," meaning Chrysler and the two major competitors. Their reasoning: When you see the difference you'll buy THEIR product. Far more powerful than the company making your decision for you. That's temporary. When the consumer makes the decision it is far more permanent. A recent Norwegian ad for

Mycron computers positioned its firm against two competitors: IBM and Norsk Data. In the ad Mycron gave you THREE coupons to request more information. One had the address of IBM the second was Norsk Data. The third was theirs! Their feeling: If "you compare all three". . . you'll buy us.

5. Ask the customers to rate your quality of service.

Stay at most major hotels around the world and there is a note asking you to "rate our service." Housekeepers are given a small reward for every filled-out report they hand in. Hotels then know what the customer wants (and they also build a database of these names). Embassy Suites does 350 in-depth customer interviews every day. "It's probably the most extensive survey ever in the hotel industry," say president Harvey Feldman.

Every week Fidelity Investor Centers in the United States asks 3,000 customers, who recently did stock market trades with them, to rate the service they received and to suggest improvements.

Cadillac gathers focus groups of owners and examines repair orders and complaints. Result: Cadillac jumped from 14th to 7th place in customer ranking of best automotive repair service.

With the NEW competition around us, today's businessman must look for innovative and different and imaginative ideas to not only keep his present customer but also have them tell others. The most effective way is through. . . direct mail advertising. HERE'S WHY: **It is far, far easier to sell more to the customer you have than to sell to a new customer.** And the way you can do that best is through direct mail advertising. This means working at it. This means taking care of the customer. This means concentrating as much on the customer you have as the customer you do NOT have. "Business is never as healthy," said Henry Ford, "as when, like a chicken, it must do a certain amount of scratching for what it gets."

Today, most of the trees on Ulawa still stand. There remain some old timers who still insist the only way they will ever come down is of you yell and scream at them. But others, younger and unwilling to be tied into old customs, have discovered you can build paths around the trees and reach the same goals.

6 What's the Color of Your Business?

My insurance salesman uses orange envelopes. When the mail arrives with the pure white stack of envelopes and an orange one is in the pile, I know I received something from my insurance agent. He also wears an orange handkerchief in his suit jacket and sometimes, for fun, orange socks. I mean, I know who *he* is. Every time. His color tells me.

What color is *your* business? Is there a specific color which, when seen, brings the name of your store to mind? There should be. It is all part of the identification process. Another technique to make you stand out (and apart) from the rest of the competition.

Our store's colors are brown and beige. So are our boxes, our bags, our stationery, even the clothes we wear. (Yes, it's also the color of Saks Fifth Avenue, but, if you get us mixed up with them, well, that's OK.)

An ad in national magazines took up two pages. One page was all copy; the other all color. The color was yellow. The headline on the copy said, "Even the color of the label separates Cutty Sark from all the rest."

You decide to buy a bottle of scotch. The salesman says, "What brand." Your eyes run over the shelf selection and you answer, "The one with the yellow label. I read somewhere it's better."

Not to be outdone, Johnny Walker Red comes back with their double page spread in **Life** magazine. More than two feet wide, with a picture of some leaves and one line of copy, the ad reads, "In the fall even the leaves turn to red."

What's that have to do with whiskey? They do not tell me the taste is better, the quality's finer, or the price is lower. All they tell me is the color of the label. Millions of dollars are spent advertising this brand (recently — a red sunset) emphasizing color.

If those colors do not make you happy with scotch you can simply choose Black and White (the ones with the two scotties on the front). Do not confuse this brand with Black Label which is Carling's beer. Then there's the Blue Ribbon of Pabst's.

My point: All these companies and advertising agencies spend all this money to make sure you identify their product with a color.

If it works for them, will it also work for you? Yes. Here's how to start. Pick a color with meaning or significance. Red can mean embarrassment (blush), a country (China), evasion (herring), delay (tape), or stop (light). White can mean Broadway (Great White Way), purity or the hats the Dodge boys wear.

Blue can mean a nursery rhyme (little boy), a painting (boy), a killer (beard), or sadness. Pink can be a state of health or a sign you are out of work. Green can be envy, inexperience, a sign to go or the pastures to lie down in. Yellow is a taxi, a coward, a sign of caution, or a ribbon tied around an old oak tree.

Gold is silence, not all that glitters, the fleece sought by Jason or the rule to guide your life.* Gray does seem to connote conservatism and age, from the suit of the same color to Geoffrey Beene's cologne or the time your mirror suggests a change to Grecian formula.

Sometimes colors become positively chameleon from the suspicious horse (the one of a different color) to the panther that was a black civil rightist in the 1960s, a pink detective in the 1970s and a gray senior citizen in the 1980s.

* Our local financial expert said the Golden Rule for bankers is simply: "Those that have the gold, rule."

Colors can also be one-word descriptions: rust (**wears** out); lemon (bad **wares**); raspberry (**where** you are criticized).

Visit your local clothing store and the descriptive colors might make you feel you walked into the fruit and produce section of your supermarket. Here are the lemons and oranges and avocados and grapes and cranberries — all colors for you to identify with and buy from.

There are the colors we associate with ethnic groups,such as the Brown Bomber before we discovered that black was beautiful.

There are firms that reach for the association— we saw a sign painted 20 stories tall recently in New York advertising: "New Newport Red" which struck us as odd because we couldn't remember the old Newport color.

You receive advertisements in the mail for White sales (sometimes towels and sheets, sometimes refrigerators and stoves). There's a paint store in Pennsylvania that advertises a "color of the month." If you are a jeweler you can have fun with gold, silver, emerald, ruby, and jade.

There's a bank in Paris that advertises itself as "the one with the yellow awnings." Not higher interest. Not faster service. Not money to loan. Simply the "color of the awnings."

Colors can be patriotic ("hooray for the red, white, and blue") or can define the purpose of going to battle ("fight under the colors").

Colors convey emotions and degrees of warmth. Blues are cool. Browns and olives are quiet, subdued, laid back, and comfortable.

Red is exciting (a good color for your next mailer) and so is purple, which is also prose andsometimes cows. As poet Gelett Burgess once wrote:

I never saw a purple cow,
I never hope to see one;
But I can tell you, anyhow,
I'd rather see than be one.

Colors have genders, or no gender. They can be masculine (black, brown, olive, beige, rust, grey, blue); feminine (pink, white, purple); or neuter (green, orange, gold, royal).

What all this means: If colors set off emotional reactions (they do), why not adapt and adopt the positive reactions for your business (you should).

When you reassociate your business with an established positive color, you have taken a giant step toward bringing your customer to read what you write and buy what you sell.

Any doubts you may have as to the success of this philosophy will disappear after the next rainfall. Simply look into the sky and see the rainbow (which is all colors) and you will remember what awaits you at the end.

7 *Saying is Believing*

In one of the first books we wrote, ("The Great Brain Robbery," co-authored with Ray Considine) we had a chapter called "Secret Selling Sentences."

This was one of them: "I have a problem and I need your help."

Soon after the book came out, someone would call at least once a week using **that** sentence on me.

"Hi, I have a problem and I need your help."

How could I **not** help? Didn't I say it worked!

Since then. . .

We have used certain phrases in our seminars or lines we thought were throw-always in this column, only to hear them return on the phone, in a letter or from a member of a seminar audience.

Here are the ones most often quoted back and that work. (Well. . . most of the time.)

1. Find out what your customer wants to buy. And give it to them.

This is the basic rule of selling. Listen to your customers when they talk to you and you will hear what they want to buy.

Stew Leonard runs one of the most successful supermarkets in the U. S. in Norwalk, Connecticut. Tom Peters lists him as an outstanding example in his book, *Passion for Excellence*. Stew will make the Guinness Book of World Records for doing more business per square foot than any store of any kind in the world! More than 100,000 people visit his store every week, and his sales are more than $100 million a year.

We visited him one day and watched him talking to customers who bought fresh flowers from his just-opened floral department. He asked if they liked the assortment. Were the prices right? Should he offer plants and flowers? All the time he was talking and they were answering, a young man stood off to the side writing down the replies. When he finished, he told the young man to have the notes typed and give them to his son, and, "Tell him that's his buying plan for tomorrow."

No statistics. No number crunching. Just talking to the customers and asking them what they wanted to buy. . .

2. Fear of loss is stronger than promise of gain.

"Win this house!" will attract readership.

"Will you lose your home this year?" will attract even more.

Author Robert Ringer says the best headline he ever wrote was for Douglas Casey's best seller, *Crisis Investing*. This was Ringer's headline: "Why you will probably lose everything in the coming depression."

The book sold more than 400,000 hardcover copies and remained in first place on *The New York Times* list for 15 weeks.

Even the **implied** fear of losing attracts. Tell the customer the exact number of a certain product you have in stock and "after they are gone, there are no more." That will make the reader stop, look, listen and think seriously about buying.

3. DWYPYWD.

We first saw this phrase used by Ray Considine and when we use it, people always ask us what it means. We first reply, "Why the letters are the same backward and forward."

"Yes," they answer, "but what does it **mean**?"

We then tell them the answer. The initials stand for: Do What You Promised You Would Do.

If you tell a customer the pants will be altered by Monday at noon, make sure they are. If you say the product or aervice will be ready to them the next day between noon and 5, make sure it is. Whatever you promise should be there in the delivery. As poet Robert Service's said in "The Burning of Sam McGee:" "A promise made is a debt unpaid."

Here's why: A recent survey revealed that 90 percent of American do not associate the word "trust" with the word "business."

What an indictment of the selling profession! But what an **opportunity** for you and your business. For if I trust you . . .I will continue to buy from you. And tell my friends to buy from you!

There are really five basic reasons people will **not** buy from you. Not trusting you is at the top of the list. (The other four are: no need, no money, no hurry and no desire.)

When asked in a study what factors influenced a buyer's purchase decision, 5,000 respondents said that number one, top of the list, was "confidence."

4. It is far, far easier to sell more to the customer you have than to sell a new customer.

What pulls best? The list of customers who shopped with you or the list of people who have not shopped with you?

Right! If you can bring a customer who shops with you four times a year back into your place of business just **one more time** each year, you have the potential of 20 percent more annual business from just that **one** customer.

Or. . .if a customer comes into your store to buy a specific item and you sell them just one more item, you are ahead.

Look at this amazing fact: American businesses spend five times as much to attract new customers than on the customers they already have!

Amazing. . .

Another plus is customer retention. The more they buy, the more they are locked in to you as their favorite business.

A survey of banking habits disclosed that if a customer had one account with a bank (say, checking), the odds against losing them are 1 to 1. If they have two accounts, the odds are 10 to 1. Three accounts, 20 to 1. And four accounts, 100 to one!

The more they buy, the more they keep coming back . . .

5. Dollar for dollar, nothing will return as much to your business as direct mail.

Next time you hear someone say, "I've tried direct mail. It doesn't work," here's your answer: "No, what you did was send something in the mail that didn't work. Now the question is what did you do? And how did you do it? And what can you do next time to make it work."

Talk to them about the importance of the list. And the offer. Talk to them about stressing customer benefits and not features. Tell them about success stories of other people in comparable businesses and how it worked for them. Because success begets success. If some idea, concept, headline brings in customers the first time, it will also bring them in a second time.

We recently did a direct mail seminar for men's clothing retailers. We asked them to send us copies of their direct mail pieces. We received one that was an exact copy of one we did for our store.

"I figured," said the store owner, "if it worked for you, it should work for me." And it did. . .

And it is true. Measure the dollars you spend for any other media — newspaper, magazine, radio, TV, billboards — and measure the response received versus the dollars spent. You will them see this sentence is true (and is its own secret selling sentence): "Dollar for dollar, nothing returns as much to your business as direct marketing."

8

Cut The Complaints And Most People Have Nothing To Say

"I went to a restaurant last night and had a terrible meal."
"I had to pull my ad at the last minute, because the manufacturer didn't ship in time."
"The post office delivered all my sale mailers — about one week after the sale started."

Listen to people talk. Hear them complain, criticize, categorize all the events that happened in their day, their year, their life. . .in a negative manner.

We use a sentence that summarizes this attitude. Here is is:

"Cut out the complaints and most people have nothing to say."

The opening quotations are good examples.

The reason for complaints is conditioning. We are all products of our environment. We copy the attitude, philosophy, and thought around us.

Listen to the conversations. Criticism of people with higher authority (the parent, the boss, the elected official).

Read the mail. A recent study showed that if customers have something bad to say about your business, they are five times more apt to write you than if they have something good to say.

Read/watch/listen to the media. Riots. Murders. Fires. Disaster. The news is overwhelmingly bad, and we are quickly conditioned to the fact that the norm is negative. This soon becomes a mind-set. We become conditioned to thinking negative. So why not think <u>positive</u> and have <u>positive</u> results?

Fact: The more we **compliment** instead of **criticize**, the greater we increase the odds of success.

A recent article in *The New York Times* quoted authorities who said the most successful transactions are those where people enter into a buyer-seller relationship in a cooperative, not a competitive frame of mind.

Working with a supplier does not guarantee success just because one pays for the service. We find ourselves enjoying our meals in restaurants far more when we compliment waiters or waitresses on their service. When we thank them for bringing the meal. When we enter into conversation with them, so they are a person and not a servant.

Where is it written paying for a service guarantees the quality of that service? Our rule of thumb is simply: What's the goal? Do we want the best service in the restaurant? Do we want the merchandise in our store? Do we want the post office to deliver mailers on time?

Then we have to start thinking of complimenting, not criticizing. We tend to think of people to whom we pay money for services as antagonists rather as partners in a common goal. ("I paid for the meal/merchandise/postage, so I should get the best possible service!" That **would** be nice. But, it simply doesn't work that way — most of the time.)

Success will come your way with much less concern, aggravation, and worry, when you start thinking of the buyer-seller exchange as opportunities for mutual gain instead of a winner-take-all philosophy. Remember the old theory in Psychology 1 that says when two people work together, it becomes the work of three. Works every time. (Well, enough of the time to start thinking of this process as an interesting alternative.)

Gwendolyn Thomas Marx, a professional singer says, "I go back to the same stores and to the same sales help in the stores where I shop. I chat. I ask how they're doing. How has their day been?" The result: "I get better service. The old hands expect me back. The new people find out I'm not someone who is going to shop there once and walk away."

How does this work in your business? Here's some ideas you might try. We did. They work.

1. Ask for help. We send a copy of our mailer with a letter to all the postmasters in the ZIP codes where our mailer will be delivered. We point out the starting date of the sale. We tell them the date the mailers should arrive at their post office. We ask them to please call us if the mailers do not arrive in time. We started this idea a few years ago. The mailing piece is not just another mailer. It is a **specific** mailer. One the postmasters are called upon to watch for. We **request** their help instead of demanding their services. Deliveries improve at once.

2. Involve Them. The more you involve a supplier or service organization with your decision-making, the more you make them responsible to do a better job for you.

This is important even if you know the right decision to make. You can give someone alternative answers to a question (any one of which is acceptable to you), and then **they** have made the decision and have a responsibility for following through.

Ask the waiter what he would recommend for the main course. And see how much more you enjoy the meal. Ask the post office what procedures you should take to guarantee quicker delivery. And watch your third-class mail move up to first-class in importance.

Ask the manufacturer for a specific date to expect the merchandise (and have **him** write down the date on your order blank), and watch the faster deliveries.

3. Compliment services. After the mailer arrives in time, we drop a note thanking the postmaster for taking care of us and helping make our sale successful.

Do the same with your manufacturers. A note thanking them for (a) prompt deliveries, (b) excellent quality, (c) superb design will find its way to the bulletin board in the delivery room or the home office. **No one** does that. People only write or call with bad news ("Cut out the complaints and most people. . .")

The next time there is a shipment to leave the factory, guess whose name will be on top of the list? The next time you need reorders on hot-selling items, guess who will receive preferential service? The next time you need a special order or service, how good is your chance for success?

What happens when customers come into your store with a "show me" attitude — where they take a superior attitude, because they are the holders of the money and you are merely the dispensers of the merchandise. Think of your attitude if they are condescending to you. Suddenly there is an adversary relationship. The question becomes one of "Who will win?" instead of "How can we **both** win?"

Now the picture changes. Now customers approach you and ask for your help. They want direction. You would know the right direction. You would know the right decision, because you deal with your merchandise on a day-by-day basis. They come to you as the expert for advice. Much as they would go to an architect to build their house, a doctor to look after their health, or a lawyer to handle their legal problems. You are the expert, they say to you. Can you help them make the right decision?

Can you? And how! "Let me show you everything we have in the store. Hold all the phone calls, I can't be disturbed. I have a very important customer."

Stop. At this point think about the difference between the average buyer of products or services who sits back and says, "I'm paying for what I ordered from my agent/supplier/ salesperson. And money talks!" It sure does. But, you'll find people don't listen as carefully as when you talk.

And ask for help.

And compliment.

And cut out the complaints.

9 Do You "Guarantee" I'll Be Happy With Your Business?

A recent nationwide survey of buyers across the United States asked the question, "Why do you buy where you buy?"

No, folks, the number one answer was NOT price. (Price was number five). The number one reason people buy where they buy is: **Confidence**. Confidence in the store. In the people. In the product.

(The other reasons in order were: Quality. Selection. Service. And THEN Price.)

People want to shop where they feel they will be taken care of. Where the quality of the product is consistent. Where what you promise is what you deliver.

Having confidence in a product is a reason why all mail order companies have guarantees in their catalogues. That's all MAIL ORDER companies. But most retailers who also do mail order do NOT offer a guarantee.

We called a few of these retailers and asked, "Why don't you have a guarantee in your catalog?" Each answered, "Our customers know us. They know we guarantee everything."

Really? We asked if they ever heard of the Curse of Assumption. A few hung up on us. Oh well . . .

And yet many retailers have this same "blind spot" in their day to day business. They "assume" their customers know who they are and what they do and why. Not true.

I bring this to your attention because I recently received a book in the mail on catalogue supplies for my store. One page, in full color was headlined: **Policy Signs Protect Your Store.**

They had illustration of these policy signs. They read as follows:

"**No** refund. Exchange ONLY."

"**No** refund or exchange on Sale Merchandise."

"NO REFUND OR EXCHANGE."

"**No** Refund after 7 days on regular priced MERCHANDISE."

Every sign began with the word "**NO.**"

What an exciting, marvelous, constructive way to inspire confidence in your store. Wherever the customer looks, they see big gold and black signs saying "NO!"

Psychologists tell you that if you have a positive attitude, it affects everyone around you. If you have a negative attitude, it affects everyone around you. Why start the day — or have all through the day, signs that say "NO!" ?

I want signs that say "YES!"

Yes, we will refund and exchange anything anytime.

Yes, we will make you happy.

Yes, we will make you satisfied.

The hot name today in retailing is Nordstrom. Nordstrom's came out of the North from Oregon to over-stored Los Angeles where everyone said "They're successful in Oregon but they'll fail in L.A. Just too many stores here." And in a few short months, they took a major share of the retail market away from the competition.

The oracles gave the same prophecy when Nordstrom's moved into Washington D.C. "They never heard of them here. It'll take years to capture a share of the market," It took. . . months. Here's why: Nordstrom customers are proselytizers who go forth in the community to spread their word and increase their sales. The stories of service to the customer are legion and by now may even be apocryphal — but they're so good they're worth repeating:

• A man called Nordstrom's because his wife died. He wanted to settle his outstanding bill. He was told it was $1,000.00 and was asked why he wanted to know.

He told them. A few days later the store wrote a letter saying his wife had been an excellent customer and he was to consider the account paid in full. (Wait, there's more!) The day of the funeral, the store sent flowers. . .

• Another man went to Nordstrom's to exchange some shirts. They were bought in another store but put in a Nordstrom box. "That's OK," said the menswear buyer, "We'll take them back for you and you can pick whatever else you want."

• The sewing of new buttons, finding of lost buttons, the dozens of extra small services show Nordstrom's knows the result of a recent consumer survey ("If you make someone happy, they'll tell three other people. If you make someone unhappy, they'll tell eleven other people.") Nordstrom's keeps the odds on THEIR side. **Confidence**.

And then there's Publix supermarkets in Florida that captures one out of every three food dollars spent in the state. They once ran an ad that was so powerful, it is now printed on the back of their calling cards. Titled "Our Guarantee" it says:

"We will never knowingly disappoint you. If, for any reason, your purchase does not give you complete satisfaction, the full purchase price will be cheerfully refunded immediately upon request. We have always believed that no sale is complete until the meal is eaten and enjoyed."

Confidence.

Since we're speaking of supermarkets. . . did you hear about the time Stew Leonard in Norwalk, Connecticut, America's best known supermarket, had a complaint from a woman who found a small piece of wood in her yogurt. The store delivered a fresh CASE of yogurt to her home! (Yes, with a written letter of apology). **Confidence**.

No wonder he'll make the Guinness book of World Records for doing more business per square foot than any store of any kind in the world.

What are we saying?

This: The techniques of Direct Mail that contribute to the growth and success of the small business — honesty, empathy, confidence — must also be carried out on the selling floor as well. Otherwise you are TWO stores working at a cross purposes.

STOP telling me what I can't do with your merchandise.

START telling me what YOU will do for me. Over and over again because you believe I am the most important person in the world: Your customer.

And if you don't believe that, ask me.

10

The Write Way To Bring In More Customers

We were glancing through bank newspaper advertising from across the country and suddenly experienced a sense of deja vu. It seemed the copy we were reading from banks in Iowa was the same copy we had just read from banks in Illinois. Which was the same copy we read from banks in Texas. Which was the same copy we read from banks in Nebraska. Which was the same copy. . .

First we thought it might be the lateness of the hour or the long arm of coincidence. Then we wondered if some Master Architect of Words had a copy-writing service subscribed to by most of the banks in the United States.

The more we read, the more we came to the conclusion it was nothing more than banks-copying-banks.

Some examples of recent bank advertising copy that doesn't work:

The Gee-We're-Great-Folks Copy:
"Helping you is our business."
"The extra money's always there when you need it."
The Gee-YOU'RE-Great-Folks Copy:
"You've worked hard for that family of yours."
The Positioning Copy:

"Our Banker's beside you." (Or "in back of you" or "we're up front.")

The What-Did-They-Say Copy:
"This account offers the ideal way to earn greater yields with the advantage of shorter term investments quarterly." (What that really means: "Deposit any amount. Your money starts making more money immediately!")

The Rent-a-Car Copy:
"Let one of our loan officers put you in the driver's seat."

The Guilt-Trip Copy:
"Show your children the special way you care for them. Plan their future with. . . "

The Homily-for-Today Copy:
"Holidays are a lot merrier when they are prepaid."

The "It-seems-to-me-I've-heard-that-song-before" Copy:
"We again offer you one of the best values in banking."

Every once in a while, however, a bank ad stands out. Separate and apart from the rest, chock-full of makes-you-want-to-read copy. With a "sound" like living room conversation with a group of friends over for the evening. Easy, comfortable, natural. That's what make good bank advertising copy.

Can advertising have interesting copy? Will people read advertising? How do you put together words and phrases that make people read your advertising — and **act** on it?

Writing good advertising copy is not difficult. There are two general rules: Do the words in your ad answer the question, "What's in it for me?" (Yes, we ask the same question about headlines, but the copy in the ad must EXPLAIN the headline.) And do the words give reasons for coming to **your** business?

You do not have to be a professional writer to "read" your ads. The consumers are not professional writers. They ARE professional readers. They scan ads quickly. If a headline in your ad captures their eye, does the copy make them keep on reading?

Question: Should the copy be long? Or short?

Answer: Whatever works.

Long copy is necessary to explain a new product. But the copy must appeal to the reader's needs. Remember the basic rule in selling: Find out what customers want and give it to them. Your job: Translate a service of your business into the needs of your customer.

Here's 10 Rules on How To Write Copy That Makes People Respond

1. **Don't exaggerate.** Tell the truth. The simple facts are very effective. They do not need embellishment. Avoid superlatives and circus adjectives ("terrific," "fantastic").

2. **Be enthusiastic.** Walter Chrysler once said he would pay more for enthusiasm than any other product. Enthusiasm is contagious — in the spoken word, in the written word.

3. **Write the whole story.** Readership falls off rapidly up to the first 50 words. But there is very little drop between 50 and 500 words. Says Dr. Charles Edwards of NYU's school of retailing: "The more facts you tell, the more you sell."

4. **Use testimonials.** Works for supermarkets, retail stores, national products, why not for you? Pictures of your customers in your ads saying why-they-like-to-buy-from-you are strong and effective.

5. **Offer advice or a service.** Some businesses offer courses on estate planning. Or energy saving. Or women's activities. Or lectures to senior citizens.

6. **Use short words,** short sentences, short paragraphs. They make your copy easy to read, understand, follow — and buy. Keep your opening paragraph down to 10 or 15 words.

7. **Take the "you" approach.** The newspaper may go to thousands of readers. Or hundreds of thousands. But the customer must feel you are writing to him alone. Use the word "you" freely. Either implied or specifically.

8. **Write naturally. Personal, warm, friendly.** A customer asks, "Is this jacket waterproof?" What do you say? Your copy should read as though someone taped the conversation and then printed it (Now that's an idea. . .)

9. Buy now. Ask for the sale. Give a reason for shopping today. The price. The selection. The limited amount. Make me want to buy. Now.

10. Every ad is an investment in your business. Each ad must stand alone, telling one story the best you can. It must be your business. Read the words aloud to yourself, to others. Does it "sound" like your business? It does? Great. You're on your way.

 # Attracting More Customers is as Easy as A-B-C

The time: August 18, 1986.

Lee Iacocca is about to address his Chrysler dealers at their annual convention in Atlantic City, N.J.

Will he announce that he is planning to run for President? Will he attack the ever-increasing national debt? Will he call for a restriction on Japanese car imports?

None of the above.

Iacocca's message was how his dealers could increase their business next year.

To succeed, he said, "All you have to do is memorize four words. Here they are. **Make someone like you.**"

His reasoning: All car agencies are alike. They all sell transportation. Shop around dealer-to-dealer and you will find the same colors, the same products and services.

Take that one step forward. Most people think all businesses are alike. Banks all sell sell financial products and services. Supermarkets all sell food. Clothing stores all sell clothing.Why should the customer choose your business over another? One reason: **They like to do business with you.**

Make one customer happy and they will tell another. Who will tell another. who, in turn, will tell another *ad profitum*.

How do you keep the odds on your side?

In 1982, American companies spent $430 million on image advertising. A few years later that figure jumped 80% to $726 million. Clearly, someone, somewhere, is concerned the message is not being heard.

And in a reverse of Marshall McLuhan's theory, the message can be the medium. Using all the media available your business can have "someone like you." It's as easy as A-B-C.

• "A" stands for **Advertising** — your window to the world. You tell everyone who you are, what you do, and why they should do business with you.

"My husband knew whom to trust," is the headline from Broadway National Bank in New York promoting its trust division under a picture of a woman contemplating her future. For added value, the bank gives the name of the person to call in its trust division, making the bank much more "personal."

Advertising: **Where you tell the customer about yourself.**

• "B" stands for **Benefits** — the reasons why a customer (and/or potential customer) will buy from you. Fort Lee Savings in New Jersey ran a headline that said it all: "The mortgage made for you: No Points!" Anyone interested in buying a house understands that benefit.

You can also benefit a specific section of the marketplace such as Women's Bank in New York City or the Women's Federal Savings Bank in Minnesota. When they first started, their name said why. Today, the name is just a name since they extend their services to the total community. But when they began, the name was an up-front benefit to the market where they positioned themselves.

And then there's Atlas Savings and Loan Association in San Francisco, which began as a financial institution run primarily by gay people for gay people.

Benefits: Where your customer tell other customers about you.

• "C" stands for **Community.** The more your business is involved with your community, the more warm feelings the community feels toward your business.

Supermarkets throughout the country are major contributors to the Special Olympics program. This involvement and commitment makes the supermarket feel good about their community. And the community feels good about the supermarket.

Community: Where everyone tells everyone else about you.

So, the next time you sit down to put together your marketing, advertising, and promotion campaign for the coming week, month, or year, remember the ABCs which stand for "**A**dvertising **B**enefits **C**ommunity." When done well, it works.

12 The Loyalty Ladder

I first saw the idea sketched on the back of a napkin in the coffee shop in Chicago's Hyatt Hotel five years ago. "It's called the 'Loyalty Ladder,' " said friend, fellow speaker and marketing consultant Ray Considine who showed me the drawing. And he showed me how it worked.

The idea is to have everyone who shops with you climb to the top of the ladder. There are five rungs and (reading from the bottom to top) they are Suspect, Prospect, Customer, Client and Advocate.

I was intrigued. We put together a version that Considine and I used. Later I modified it to become part of my all-day direct marketing program.

The idea soon caught on. Other speakers and writers who heard the concept picked it up and began to use it themselves.

- During a recent trip to New Zealand, we saw where the marketing people for Beecham's laboratories took the idea and adopted and adapted the concept for the relationship between their company and their pharmacists.

- Marketeer John Groman from Epsilon in Cambridge, Massachusetts, put together his **own** Loyalty Ladder for fund raising. John's ladder has *six* rungs: Awareness, Interest, Support, Commitment, Involvement and Legacy. (Hey, listen . . . whatever works!)

Recent how-to direct mail videos include the Loyalty Ladder. It has been reprinted in books, magazine articles and video presentations.

I asked Considine where he first heard of the idea. He told me he heard about it from Ray Cusato in California. Cusato conducts training workshops in areas involving the customer. Was he the first person to use the Loyalty Ladder?

No, said Cusato, he worked on the idea with Walter Geyer in New York City back in 1976. The two of them were doing a workshop for International Paper. "Here's five steps for salespeople to use to increase sales in their territory," said Geyer.

Cusato works the program as a funnel rather than a ladder. "It works better for me that way," he says, "with most of the people at the big end and then filtering down to the few who become advocates."

OK, you're asking by now (well, we hope you're asking by now), **What is the Loyalty Ladder?** And how does it work? On the next page we show you the transition from suspect to advocate on the Loyalty Ladder.

Suspect: Someone who could possibly buy your product or service.

"Are you kidding Murray? Do you know how expensive it is to advertise? I have a tough enough time putting together money for local advertising much less everyone who could possibly buy my merchandise."

Well, you're right. So let's move up to the next step of the ladder.

Prospect: Someone who has heard about you but hasn't yet bought from you.

They've heard about you. Read about you. Someone recommended you. They know who you are, where you are and what you sell. But they still haven't come to shop with you.

Customer: Someone who has bought from you at least one time.

But they can be a customer of yours and also a customer of your competition as well.)

Client: Someone that buys everything you have to offer that they could possibly want.

"Wait a minute. If someone is buying everything from me that they can possibly use, how could anything be better than that?"

There is one more step of the ladder. At the very top: THE ADVOCATE.

Advocate: Someone who tells everyone else to buy from you.

The advocate is someone who is so happy with what they are buying from you that they become disciples. When new people come into town and are looking to buy a particular product, this person brings them directly to you and says, "I want you to take care these folks the same way you take care of me!" That is what an advocate is — someone who goes around town bringing customers to you.

13 Say Hello To Your Most Expensive Salesperson

You spend very little time with him. You often let him make decisions that affect your business while spending only a few minutes discussing his thoughts, directions, and ideas.

He has become, through the years, the spokesperson for you and yet you spend less time with him on a weekly basis than you do on a customer taking out a loan or buying a pair of socks or selecting food for dinner.

When he tries promotions for your business, new products, he often succeeds but as often fails. But no one takes the time to sit down and examine reasons why or what to avoid next time.

He has become one of your most expensive employees and yet takes the smallest amount of your time.

His name: **Your Advertising.**

In a large business this lack of attention does not happen because the giants have advertising departments and advertising agencies and each work with one another on a full time basis.

But most small businesses do not have this luxury of time and dollars.

Many small businesses have additional responsibilities from buying supplies to opening the door in the morning to answering questions like, "How come someone's in my parking space?"

Are there simple easy-to-follow rules to help, assist, guide you in your day-to-day planning and coming up with new ideas?

Yes. It begins with Stop, Look and Listen.

STOP! Look at your daily/weekly/annual advertising schedule. STOP what you are doing right now and look around your office for that calendar on your wall. Do you have a promotion scheduled every month? You should. Tie into holidays (There's one every month except August).

You have to stop. . . before you start.

You have to decide what has to be done when.

You have to put together a plan IN ADVANCE as to what merchandise you will promote when.

LOOK at what's happening in industry: Set aside one morning a week for a few hours. Someone else answers the phone (and takes all messages because you always return calls). Make believe you are at a special meeting because you are. It's a marketing/learning/observing getting ideas meeting.

Make sure you read the weekly newspapers. The monthly magazines. See what other businesses like yours are doing you can adopt and adapt for YOUR business.

LISTEN to what's happening all around you. One of the best places: seminars and cassettes in the car.

OK, now that you know how to gather up your ideas, how do you find your own ideas?

That was the same question facing James Webb Young in 1928 as vice president of J. Walter Thompson. He had taken this company and made it a world leader. One day a magazine editor called and asked since Young was so successful he must have a secret formula for coming up with ideas. Would he share it with the magazine's readers?

Webb was startled. He never thought about having "a secret formula." He told the editor that ideas just seem "to come to mind" but that he would think about it and return his call.

He did. And out of that brief conversation came a small book called *The Technique of Producing Ideas* that has become so well known that it is the rare advertising symposium where some speaker does NOT say, "As James Webb Young said, in 'The Technique of Producing Ideas. . .'"

Here then, in capsule form, are his five steps to **"produce ideas."**

1. Gather the raw material. Facts that relate to the product and the people you want to buy that product. Put them down on 3 x 5 ruled cards. List one item to a card.

2. Think about it. Read what you have written. "Listen" for the results of the creative process — DO NOT "look" for the answer. As you think about it, partial ideas will come to you. Put those down on paper (no matter how crazy or incomplete). They are the foreshadowings of the real idea that is coming down the line.

3. Forget about it. No conscious effort to remember. Drop the whole subject. Here's what you are really doing: Turning the ideas over to your subconscious mind and letting it work while you sleep. Do something else. Listen to music. Go to the theatre or movies. Read.

4. Be ready for the answer. Suddenly the way to promote, advertise, market your idea comes to you! While sleeping. When waking up. While working. Suddenly, somewhere, somehow, it happens. Don't look for it. It will suddenly . . . just appear.

5. Shape it up. Now you have it, show it to others. Shape and develop the concept so that it works. "A good idea," said Young, "has self expanding qualities. It stimulates those who see it to add to it."

Will this simple but effective method work for you?

Yes.

Part Two

Targeting Your Customer

14

Acres of Diamonds

At the turn of the century, a minister by the name of Dr. Russell Conwell traveled throughout the United States and gave the same speech nearly 6,000 times. The effect was so powerful that wherever he went, audiences would pack the halls to hear him talk. He earned several million dollars (a huge amount of money for that time) and donated the proceeds to found Temple University in Philadelphia.

His speech was titled, "Acres of Diamonds." His theme: "Diamonds are not in far-distant mountains or in yonder seas: They are in your own back yard, if you just dig for them. . . "

This is the story of how that sermon still works today in any business if the merchant simply uses direct mail — a tool that will prove to any and every business man and woman that there are, literally, "Acres of Diamonds" in their own back yards. . .

We call our Diamond (or yours), the "Data Base Diamond." Here are the four files that make up the Data Base Diamond:

1. The Prospect File.
2. The Customer File.
3. The Suppression File.
4. The Store File.

Each file has three parts. Let's take them one at a time. . .

THE PROSPECT FILE

Your future customers are right in your own back yard. All you have to do is go out and dig them up. Three key places to look are voting lists, ZIP codes and list brokers. Select from these lists the ones that most closely match your customer profile. These are your best prospects for increased growth.

Part One

Voting Lists — Leo McGinley & Sons market in Falcarragh, Ireland, decided they would try direct mail, but there were no list brokers and no mailing lists. But there WAS a list of voters in the town — each a potential McGinley customer. And so he sent his very first mailer to the 5,000 voters (households) announcing a special sale on Mother's day. Since the holiday fell on a Sunday, they received permission from the parish priest to open that day.

The results were more than the store could handle. Nearly half the population of the town showed up for the sale. Not only did the small police force have to come to handle the crowd, but the parish priest had to be called to calm the crowd.

The mailer cost $4,000. Business done: $52,000. And they won an ECHO Award for outstanding direct mail.

Part Two

Zip Codes — The Norman Eton Street Station, a restaurant chain in Michigan, sent a laser mailing to 40,000 customers. They selected ZIP codes of people with incomes over $30,000 (most retailers would know income levels by where people live) and businesses with more than 10 employees. They enclosed a personalized check redeemable for several different reduced-price meal offers. They matched ZIP codes to income areas of potential customers.

Cost of mailer: $20,000. Response rate: 40 percent, for a business total of $368,000!

Part Three

List Brokers — Norm Thompson is a catalog company in the Northwestern United States. To increase its mailing list, they did an analysis of their customers. The demographic results were matched against a profile of readers of U. S. magazines. They asked list brokers to find a magazine whose readers' lifestyle most closely matched current Norm Thompson customers. The company ran an ad in that magazine offering a free pair of socks (value: $6) to anyone who simply wrote and asked for a pair.

More than 300,000 orders were received. **And, nearly 20 percent were converted to full-time customers!** That's 60,000 orders.

Why? The company simply reached out to list brokers to build more customers based on the customers they presently had.

THE CUSTOMER FILE

This file is divided into three groups:

A) **A listing** of which customers bought what, where, when and how.

B) **Where customers live,** how much they earn, what kind of car they drive (demographics, geographics).

C) **All customers.**

The Listing — At one time, our store sent **every** mailing to everyone on our mailing list. Thousands and thousands of mailing pieces. But, what if. . . we had a list of which customers bought what merchandise? And we did! Our computer could pull off, by department and kind of merchandise, specific customers' names on address labels.

Now, for a cost of only a few hundred dollars (because the lists were in the hundreds instead of thousands), we were able to produce mailing pieces quickly and inexpensively with a high return (30 to 40 percent) because the mailers went to customers with a history of buying the merchandise we were offering.

The Demographic/Geographics — MBank Preston is the largest suburban bank in Dallas in the richest area, where the average home value is $400,000.

Question: What do high-income buyers look for when investing their money?

Answer: The highest interest they can find.

MBank Preston took these two ingredients — high interest and high income — and combined them in a marketing campaign for Individual Retirement Accounts (IRAs).

They pinpointed their advertising to three ZIP codes in the Dallas area right in the location of all those $400,000 (and higher) homes.

They promoted the IRAs in general advertising but pinpointed the three ZIP codes in mailings.

Results: 65 percent of their business came from the three ZIP codes. The balance came from other 55 ZIP codes in Dallas.

Each new IRA customer received a personal letter from the bank's chairman of the board.

Total budget was $53,000. The campaign brought in $7 million in IRAs and 40 percent was from new customers because the banks dug for gold in the hills where it was buried.

All Your Customers — Our store has an annual sale on New Year's Day. This mailing goes to the **total** mailing list.
• No other stores are open.
• Gordon's is only open for four hours.
• The sale is advertised only by direct mail.

And again, this year as in the past 25 consecutive years, our store did more business in these four hours on this one day than it did in most WEEKS of the year!

By carefully segmenting a business' database and, when appropriate, using the entire database for specific offers, businesses will soon discover they have, in their own back yard, Acres of Diamonds.

All they have to do is go dig them up.

THE SUPPRESSION FILE

How many names do you have on your mailing list that you shouldn't have on your mailing list? What customers have moved? Where? Should they still receive your mail? What customers have a limit on their credit? What old customers do you want to become active one more time? Here's the three parts of this file:

1. Returned mail.
2. Credit risks.
3. Recapturing old customers.

Let's take them one at a time.

Returned Mail — Nearly one out of five people in your community move every year. Some die. Some are born. Some move in. Some move out. Print the phrase "Address Correction Requested" on the bottom of your mailer. For a small fee, the post office returns your mailers with corrected addresses of customers who have moved. Now you have the choice of sending your advertisement to the new address, or not sending it at all ("Aha, they moved to California. Well, they probably won't come 3,000 miles for my sale. . .").

Credit Risks — You have customers who do not pay their bills on time or do not pay them at all. You certainly do not want to encourage then to come in and charge more!

"Suppression" means just that: taking such names OFF your mailing list because you would otherwise compound an existing problem.

Recapturing Old Customers — Every store has customers who have not shopped for a certain period of time. Surveys show nearly seven out 10 of these customers did not come back "for no particular reason."

Direct mail says, you **want** them to come back. One very simple tool is a gift certificate mailed to these customers offering them $5 or $10 off their next purchase. No minimum purchase. No gimmicks. Nothing up your sleeve. After all, you are going to your customers. (No, you would not put an ad in the newspaper saying you will give the first $10 free to **anyone**. You are offering the money to **someone** — your customer!)

For the small cost of printing and postage, you will receive back 10 to 20 times your investment (or more) because you simply showed your customers you care about them. (As an owner of a children's store in Sweden puts it: "Direct mail is an extension of kindness to our customers.")

Suppression also means making sure you do not eliminate certain customers.

THE STORE FILE

We use our customer list to find out more information about our store, the departments, what's selling what to whom, and when.

The Store File has three parts:
1. Loyalty building.
2. How's each department doing?
3. Response. Results. Analysis.

Loyalty — One way for your store to do more business is to have your customers shop more often. If you have customers who only buy a certain designer, why not send this narrow list a mailing piece about that designer's just-arrived merchandise and/or sale? Cost is small. Returns are high. What you've done is pinpoint a very small section of your mailing list with a high buying power.

Translate this to customers who buy hi-fi components, vintage wines, lawn care products. Whatever your business, you have a tight cadre of loyal customers that want to be told you have something special for them.

Response. Results. Analysis. — Some supermarkets in the United States give plastic cards to their customers with the customer's name and individual bar code on the plastic.

Now, when the customers come into the store and show their card at the point of purchase, it is passed over the scanning machine, just like the products they buy.

Now, the store knows at the end of any given period which customers bought a lot of meat ("We sent you this mailing because you are a good customer of our meat products. And we've enclosed some special coupons on meat products. . . "), or fish. . . or anything. Perhaps you want the computer to give you a list of names and addresses of customers that have not shopped in the past 30 days. You can contact them with a special inducement to make them come back one more time.

15

A Jug of Wine,
A Loaf of Bread
and DM

A jug of wine

Business was off in Russell Taylor's liquor store in Bonar Bridge, Scotland.

Here it was just before Christmas and New Year's and business was **off**! Not just for him but his neighbors as well. They reported volume drops of 25 to 30 percent from the previous year.

"If only there was a way," said Taylor, "I could let my regular customers know about the good prices I have in my Bridge Bottle Shop. Why the people would certainly come and buy from me. . ."

And so, while his fellow shopkeepers on the street stood by their doorways and waited for their customers to arrive. (And waited. And waited.). . . Russell Taylor started writing letters.

There are only 640 households in Bonar Bridge. Taylor wrote to them all.

His letter was typewritten with little hand written notes in blue ink scattered throughout the copy.

He began with, "No need to go to the ends of the earth to get bargains in booze," and then inserted in blue ink, "or even to Inverness. . ."

He listed what he sold, the special prices, little written asides ("and there are more reduced prices in the store") and ended with a handwritten, "Have a cheerful Christmas and a prosperous New Year."

He added a P.S. saying all purchases would be gift wrapped free.

Here's what happened in Taylor's words:

"While the other businesses in town did much less, I increased my business **60 percent** over the previous year."

Taylor is now sending "thank you" postcards to his customers after they buy. He says this small gesture has "already paid off with customers calling to thank me for my card and then give me extra business I never would have had."

"I used to think I would do better business anywhere except where I am here in Bonar Bridge in the Scottish Highlands. But Direct Mail has proven otherwise. . ."

A Loaf of Bread. . .

When Norman Gordon opened his Alley Deli restaurant in Atlantic City, New Jersey he had a nostalgic, turn-of-the century decor, new kitchen, new tables and chairs, an exciting, well-priced menu. Everything you need to start a successful new restaurant. Except customers.

There were the few that wandered in from the next door shopping center. But not enough . . .

How, with a limited budget, could he have people make that all-important first visit? And, having arrived, return again and again because of his high quality and low prices.

Direct Mail!

He sent a letter to all the VIP's in the community. To the main partner in law firms. To the mayor, chief of police, county executive heads of all the city and county offices located in buildings just a few blocks away from his restaurant.

His purpose was twofold:

1. To have the reader come to his Alley Deli for lunch.
2. To have the reader call the Alley Deli to have lunch delivered.

The letter was addressed to each individual by name and included a copy of the menu. This was the headline:

"Whoever Said There's No Such Thing As A Free Lunch Didn't Know About This Letter."

The first sentence said who he was ("My name is Norman Gordon") and what he did ("I just opened the Alley Deli. . . ")

He then gave a brief description of his restaurant and invited the reader to join a new exclusive group called, "The Taster's Club."

He explained there was no dues, no meetings. All you had to do to belong was accept a **free** lunch.

He ended by saying he would call in a few days for the order they would choose from his enclosed menu.

Total mailing was to 120 people. Here's what happened:

- More than 100 accepted the free lunch.
- More than half ordered at least **one additional** lunch at the same time.
- About 75 came in person within a week after the free lunch was delivered. Most are now steady customers either in person or over the phone.

For an investment of less than $225 ($25 in postage and $200 in actual food costs) he built a steady and growing sit-down and take-out business.

He says, "It would have taken me six months to bring in the kind of business direct mail brought me in six days. And I couldn't afford to wait six months. . ."

In the three years since he wrote his original letter, Gordon has tripled the size of his restaurant. And there is still a line waiting to be seated during the busy lunch hour.

Yes, the food is good, the selection interesting. The quantity is sufficient and the prices reasonable. But the fact remains this is a business that was successful on opening day and continued to be successful because of. . . Direct Mail.

P. S. — In the past three years the Alley Deli has done <u>no</u> other advertising. But they are presently experimenting with sending daily fax notices to their best customers with "Today's Specials. Call by 11 am and we'll deliver by noon!" And it works. . .

P. P. S. — The Alley Deli letter was selected by author Richard S. Hodgson in his recent book, "The Greatest Direct Mail Letters Of All Time."

16

Gonna Sit Right Down and Write Myself a Letter

The bank was one of the smallest in New York City, and it wanted to increase deposits.

Chelsea National Bank President Merton Corn knew what he could not do. He could not afford to advertise on TV. He could not afford to advertise in the New York Times. He could not afford to advertise on the New York radio stations' top-rated drive time. He could not afford to advertise in New York magazines.

He could, however, afford direct mail.

Corn drew a circle around his bank located on the map just below Central Park, and said this "community" of about 30 blocks within the circle was the "city" where his bank was located. Then he began his direct marketing advertising campaign.

He put together a series of letters, each aimed at a different market.

• **Firefighters and police officers.** Why not deposit their checks in the nearby Chelsea Bank, suggested one letter.

• **Current depositors.** Other letters offered incentives if they opened additional accounts with the bank.

• **Corporate personal accounts.** Corn wrote to companies that borrowed from the bank for their businesses, asking for their personal accounts.

- **President to president.** In letters to the small businesses in his newly formed "circle city," Corn opened with, "You're the president of a small business. I'm the president of a small bank. Why don't we get together and talk president to president?"

Business jumped at the Chelsea Bank in both dollars and customers all because of an advertising campaign that was limited to . . . the writing of letters.

Writing a letter is the simplest form of direct mail. It is the definition of direct mail. The letter is mailed directly to your customers.

Direct mail shows your customer you care.

Direct mail is the medium that shows your strong points: friendliness, reliability, service, and most important, the amount of personal attention lavished on the customer.

It is not complicated. Sit down and write a letter to your customers as if you were writing a letter to yourself. Make it chatty, informal, comfortable and newsworthy.

That means you do not begin with the time-honored and boring sentences:

"In response to your letter of the 13th. . ."

"Pursuant to your notification of employment opportunities. . ."

"I am in receipt of your letter. . . "

Begin with something to capture the reader's attention and interest. A story. A saying. An offer. A something that will make them stop and read.

Ask yourself if your letter passes the stop, look, and listen test.

Stop

You can't write a letter until you first know what you want to accomplish. Write down, in one sentence, what you want your finished letter to do.

Your letter, like a story, a play, a speech, has three parts: (1) a beginning, (2) a middle, and (3) an end.

Your letter should follow these three steps in a logical sequence. Your beginning should make a dramatic statement ("What will happen to me if I read this?"). Your middle explains in more detail what you just said ("Oh, so that's what they mean"). And reinforces your basic selling point ("Hmmmm, look what happened to others who bought this,") Your end persuades and finally convinces ("Quick, where's my pen to fill in this order blank").

Having your letter follow a regular, organized presentation makes it easier for the customer to follow along.

But you cannot start until you first **Stop**. Ask yourself: What do I want the reader to do after they read this letter?

Look

What does your letter "look" like? If you write one long paragraph to fill each page, the letter is not too attractive to look at, much less to read.

Keep your sentences short. Keep words to one or two syllables. Keep paragraphs to two or three sentences.

Avoid adjectives. Use action verbs. Eliminate unnecessary words that slow down the reader like "that". . . "a". . . "an."

Listen

After you have finished writing your letter, read it aloud. "Listen" to it as though you were someone who received it rather than wrote it.

All the direct mail rule books say, "Write as though you were talking." Or, "Write a letter to your Aunt Minny."

Listen to the arguments you make for buying in your letter. Would they convince you? Have you anticipated your readers' questions/objections and come up with answers? Have you given them enough information to buy?

Are you writing as if you were writing to one person and not to your hundreds or thousands or tens of thousands of customers?

Use "connector" words like "and," "or," "but." Those are words people use when they talk. So use those words when you write.

Stop. Sit down. Decide what you're going to say. How you're going to say it. what you want to leave in and leave out.

Look. Does the letter "look" interesting to read?

Listen. How does it "sound" to you? Does it give a clarion call to buy?

Steps to a Successful Letter

Why do some letters work and other do not?

One accepted technique is explained by direct marketing expert Bob Stone in his excellent book, "Successful Direct Marketing Methods." He says, "This is a letter-writing formula that has served me well."

1. Promise a benefit. Up front. Right in the beginning. Award-winning copywriter Bill Jayme asks, "Does the lead on your letter say 'Read me because. . .'?"

What positive event will happen to the reader who keeps on reading?

2. Enlarge on the benefit. The opening benefit is short, concise, summarized. It could be a headline on the top of the letter. It could be a strong, attention-demanding first paragraph.

Now, the next few paragraphs explain in greater detail what is included in this benefit.

3. Be specific. Tell how much money they will actually have at the end of an actual time. Money, not percentages. The more specific you are, the more real the benefit appears.

4. Give proof. Testimonials are good. Names of your customers and their positive comments are good examples of the strength of word-of-mouth advertising.

5. What happens if they don't act. Remember fear of loss is greater than promise of gain. That's why there is so much insurance sold. And that is the reason cut-off dates are important in your letter. Spur the customer to immediate action.

6. Repeat. The close of the sale. Where the salesperson summarizes and repeats all the benefits of buying he listed during the entire sales talk. Short, concise. And gives reason for buying. . . now!

7. AFTO. The salesperson's critical concluding phrase: Ask For The Order.

Tell the customer what to do. "Cut along this line." "Print your name here." "Fold and seal." Etc. . .

Remember: Direct mail is a very special relationship between you and your customer. It is a me-and-thee approach. It is the two of you sharing some information.

And it starts with you simply, sitting down and. . . writing a letter.

17 The Face is Familiar But I Can't Recall the Name

Within the past few months I bought a $5,000 air conditioner, a $600 TV set, a $7,000 car and a $50 pair of shoes.

Following these sales, I heard from none of the businesses — except my shoe salesman. He thanked me for coming in to buy and hoped I would "receive much comfort" and to remember him the next time I wanted another pair of shoes. Or perhaps had a friend who. . .

There's something wrong here.

I called each of the retailers (except the shoe store) and asked if they ever thought of writing thank-you letters after the sale. These are the actual answers:

The Air Conditioner Dealer: "I don't think we ever did that. Well, once in a while our financing company writes a letter to all the people they carry on their books." (What for? He wasn't sure.) "Listen, we know it's a good idea and I know you're going to ask why we don't do it, and the answer is, I guess we just never got around to it. There's so much to do in this business. . ."

The Television Dealer: "Sending a thank you letter is the best thing we ever did. Absolutely. We stopped about eight or nine months ago. We're so backed up with all the paper work in warranties and finance deals that we just don't have the time anymore. But I'll tell you something — from the customer's point of view it was terrific. We used to get a big response. We have to get back to that sometime. . . "

The Automobile Dealer: "Are you kidding? Why that's the first thing we do. The day the car is delivered, the salesman sits down and writes a thank you letter right away. Positively. . ."

Well, that was a month ago. No letter yet.

What's happening?

The independent small retailer — who sells about 80 percent of the consumer goods is this country — is in the best position he could hope for in many years because today's consumer is disenchanted with the large chain's "Big Is Better" philosophy. Retailing has turned full circle and the buzz words of successful businesses are, once again, "fun. . .enjoyment. . .service. . .taking care of the customer." Giant conglomerates are having difficulty with their balance sheets. Where are all those people in customerland spending their dollars?

In the smaller, neighborhood, independent-owned store.

Especially if the smaller, neighborhood, independent-owned store shows the customer they appreciate their business.

Certainly no form of merchandising or advertising ingenuity can replace the power and strength of direct mail for increasing this business.

It is a generally ignored fact of retailing that is far, far easier to sell more to the customer you have than to sell a new customer.

How do you do that? One way! Direct mail.

The retailer, complaining he is so busy doing other things he "just doesn't have the time," falls into the trap of worrying so much about his store that he forgets about his customer. It is the old make-work syndrome. Work expands in relationship to the time allotted. If you have a one hour job but you also have three hours to finish the job, the job becomes a three hour job.

"But I don't have the time. . ." is really an excuse for "I haven't figured out how to do that in my daily schedule."

It is not difficult. There are easy 1-2-3 steps:

1. Write the customer's name, address and zip code on sales slips. If you are an automobile dealer you have this information. If you are an appliance dealer you have the name on the sales/delivery slip. If you are a ready-to-wear retailer take the name when the sale is made.

2. Hire someone to type these addresses on envelopes. . . daily! This saves the salesperson time. It can be a high school student after school. It can be someone in the office you can spare for a daily hour or two — that's all it takes. This must be done daily. Otherwise the lists pile up. Return the typed envelope to the person who made the sale with a small reminder on what-was-sold.

3. The salesperson writes a thank you note. Daily. In her handwriting. On memo paper you supply. A simple two or three sentence "Thanks for coming in to see us. Hope you enjoy using your (name of product). If you have any questions or need more information on (name of product) please call me." And includes her calling card.

Maintaining this contact will surprise and flatter most customers. They will show your letter to others and say, "How about that!" Because it is unusual in today's competitive retailing world to remember the reason you are in business: To pay attention to your customer. And not what other retailers are doing.

The path to success starts with these simple "thank you" notes. You are, of course, also building lists for future sales. If your store sells appliances you might consider writing the customer who just bought an air conditioner or TV about a special promotion of refrigerators or toaster ovens or radio clocks or popular price small appliances for Christmas.

Or how about Father's Day, or Mother's Day. Most people wait until the last minute before they buy for special occasions. A memo from you will remind them and offer gift-giving solutions.

Our local florist recently celebrated his 100th year in business. He has one person responsible to send out reminders on who-sent-what-to-whom last year at this time and the florist will be glad to repeat the order if you simply call. . .

No wonder he's still doing business after 100 years. The customer contact that made him successful through the years still works.

A few months ago, coming back from an International Marketing Seminar in Switzerland, this writer chatted with a magazine publisher about direct marketing and the small retailer.

"They still haven't learned, have they?" said the publisher. "What will it take to show store owners the vast, unexplored and potentially profitable route available to them by simply using direct mail?"

"Oh," we said confidently, "they're learning. They're catching on. After all, everyone wants to do more business. . ."

Except, of course, the air conditioner dealer, the television dealer and the automobile dealer in my home town.

18

The Ten Golden Rules To Keep Them Reading

Here are some techniques to follow when writing your next direct mail piece to your customer to make them aware of who you are, what you are and why they should buy your product. We call these guidelines: *The Ten Golden Rules to Grab Attention, Hold Interest and Influence Action.*

1. Start with a question (or your strongest benefit).

"Are you the type of person who. . . "

"What would you say if. . . "

"Would you buy a $ 50 shirt for $ 29.99?"

Those are the kind of headlines that begin letters and are read. By asking a question up front, the customer is pulled into the copy wanting to find the answer. Particularly if the question is universal enough to apply to anyone— or, even better, a specific question that deals with a specific business.

2. Make it newsworthy.

Work your copy around a recent newspaper article of interest to your reader. If the article is from the *Wall Street Journal* or the *New York Times* and your audience is a businessman, you have made him first curious, then inquisitive, then reading, and then (hopefully) a buyer.

3. Make it specific.

Don't write in generalities. Relate to me. . . or my problem. Pinpoint your words: "Here's how 14 inches of floor space can return $30,000 a year. . . in profit." That's specific! All the way through. And readable.

4. Identify with the needs of the reader—quickly!

Don't wait until the third paragraph to mention a subject of interest to the reader. He will probably never make it down that far. His interest should be up-front. Try for the first sentence. At least the first paragraph.

Readership surveys show a person's attention falls off during the first 50 words. But if they read up to that point, they will read the next 500 words.

5. Emphasize benefits, not selling points.

Remember the "What's in it for me" philosophy. Instead of showing how easy you can make the premium payments of a life insurance policy, why not say, "When you're 30,000 feet in the air, your wife is taken care of." Talk about how your product works to *their* advantage (i.e., more sales, more profit, more warehouse turns, less inventory, less personnel, energy saving. .)

6. Write towards the present tense.

Avoid the past perfect tense. Work your sentences as close to the present tense as possible. Makes everything seem more immediate.

7. Make the words suit the action.

If you are writing to professionals, don't write "Zippy-do-dah-yesssiree, baby" copy. Don't write circus adjectives ("terrific," "fantastic," "extraordinary").

And yes, before you ask, if you are writing to sell tickets for a carnival or circus use the circus adjectives simply because you are. . . "making the words suit the action."

8. Use subheads to keep them reading.

Too much type in close cramped quarters make it difficult to read. Separate your paragraphs with (a) white space, and (b) subheads that keep the reader reading because the subheads provoke interest. Newspapers do this in their typesetting. You should do the same in your typewriting.

9. Use short, punchy, dramatic, attractive, effective words and punctuation.

Understand? Make sentences easy-to-read. Keep them short. Keep paragraphs short. Like this one. Holds interest. Keeps readers reading. . .

10. Write with E's Emotional, Enthusiastic, Entertaining and Easy-to-read.

Everyone like to hear a storyteller, From the time of the caveman to cowboys resting at night to tales around the campfire we heard in summer camp. What made them interesting? They were told with fervor, excitement and we were caught up in the moment.

A good selling letter should have these same qualities.

Even if the busy executive never sees your envelope and appreciates the effort and talent you assembled to create this original interest, your finished letter in his desk will be read. If you remember to write with ease. Make that E's. . .

19 Which Came First: The Chicken Or The Egg?

One way to get rid of the competition is to start a fire and burn them. That was the solution decided by small businesses throughout the United States at the turn of the century.

A new competitor had arrived, unannounced, into thousands of small communities throughout the country. Young men from the towns were enlisted and paid 10 cents apiece to buy each member of the competitor's salesforce and toss them into a giant bonfire held in the town square.

The new competitor's name: Mail Order. And the "salesmen" burned in the giant bonfire in the town square were catalogs stolen from mailboxes.

The victim was Montgomery Ward, a retailer turned mail order firm, from the big city of Chicago. Ward's very presence scared the business community into a flaming fight for their survival.

Today, 75 years later, that one catalog in the mailbox per family per year has grown to 75 catalogs per family per year.

In 1972 there were only a dozen major catalogs in the United States.

Today there are more than 7,000!

In just a few years, the printing and mailing of catalogs doubled from 4 billion a year to 8 billion a year.

Suddenly the field is overcrowded.

Suddenly there are cries of "catalog glut."

And suddenly the catalogs have found a new, different and original way to sell their merchandise: Open a store!

The wheel has turned full circle. The cataloger has decided to also be a retailer.

And, to further complicate matters, the retailer seeing the dollars pulled off his street by mail order has decided to become a cataloger!

And so today the question is: Which came first? The chicken or the egg.

- The retailer who decided to become a cataloger?
- Or the cataloger who decided to become a retailer?

The answer, as in all these types of hypothetical conundrums is. . . both.

Some retailers own both chickens and eggs. One example: Bloomingdale's department store. Their Bloomingdale's-By-Mail division is a separate entity from their retail operation with a separate fulfillment division in a separate state.

The catalog is mailed to you only if you either (1) Ask them from their space ads in magazines or (2) You fit into the demographic profile lists they rent.

They started five years ago with 12,000 customers. Today they have 1 million people who buy!

"If you haven't ordered by the time you receive our third catalog, you're off our list," says director Dianne Dunne.

Half their orders are by mail, half by phone—and the total catalog sales add up to the second highest volume "store" of their entire chain.

Looking through the Bloomingdale's catalogs, you soon see the emergence of three evolutionary changes in catalogs that are spreading to the entire mail order industry.

1. It's not free. You pay. "We first offered it free," says Dunne, "then we offered it at a price. We found out the customer who pays buys more." Cost to the customer for each catalog: $3. Or a subscription for $15.

Gucci's catalog costs $5 and can be found on newsstands and in bookstores.

Frederick's of Hollywood catalog featuring intimate lingerie (which they title "Sinsational") sells for $3 — about the same price as Playboy — and is just as interesting to look through.

2. Paid advertising. The idea started with Harrods in London, jumped across the channel to Hermes in Paris then leaped across the ocean to America. Ads for non-competitive products (liquor, automobiles) are found in catalogs that not only match the demographics of the customer, but also help pay printing and postage.

3. Has a "magazine" look. Some observers call these "new" catalogs "Magalogues" or "Catazines" because they combine mail order with the appearance of a magazine on your local newsstand.

A Lands End catalog included a special short story on the relationship between a father and his son that had nothing to do with the merchandise offered for sale. A Gucci's catalog is a "work of art in its own right," said their marketing and retail operations officer. The photography is by Milanese cameraman Fabrizio Ferri. A Bloomingdale's-By-Mail catalog featured the work of five international photographers: Scavullo, Parkinson, Horst, Turbeville and Meola.

At this point, let's stop for a minute and focus on a good example of retailer-turned-cataloger who was — and is — successful in both areas; someone who knew all the tricks, techniques and target marketing the experts say you must know and do to succeed.

The name of the company is L.L. Bean. They are located in the small town of Freeport, Maine. A team of marketing analysts once put together a group of L.L. Bean mail customers and asked them what they thought about when someone said "L.L. Bean."

One woman answered, "I see a small log cabin. There's a light in the window. The snow is falling. It is beautiful and calm."

Well, Abraham Lincoln was born in a log cabin. But not L.L. Bean. But such is the perception from which images are made.

Bean founded his business on the second floor of a downtown building in Freeport, right above the post office. A rather startling coincidence since this same post office would one day be the catalyst for not only sending out Bean catalogs, but also receiving orders for Bean merchandise.

Although the town's population is only 7,000, more than 2 million people come to shop L.L. Bean every year. The store is open 24 hours a day 365 days of the year, and does $40 million in sales—about $1,000 a square foot (nearly 10 times the normal volume of department stores).

Add to this figure an additional $220 million L.L. Bean does in mail order and you see why they are a perfect chegg (which is a combination of both chicken and egg).

Leonard Bean was 40 years old when he went into business. His early years were spent selling soap door-to-door, trapping and hunting.

When he went duck hunting in the marshes, his shoes got wet. He cut off the bottom of a pair of leather boots and sewed on a pair of rubbers for soles. It seemed to work. He sold 100 pairs to other hunters.

In a few weeks 90 pairs came back because the soles separated from the uppers. He made good on every pair and went to U. S. Rubber Company. They designed a vulcanized sole which was and is the basis for the company's success: the Maine Hunting Shoe. It is still his best selling item; with more than 200,000 pairs sold every year.

He opened his first retail store in 1917. In 1924 he employed 25 people. Today they employ 1,700 people. Their modern warehouse covers half a million square feet and fills up merchandise shipped all over the world.

His philosophy was, and is, very simple: "Sell good merchandise at a reasonable profit, treat your customers like human beings and they'll always come back for more."

L.L. died in 1967 at the age of 94. His grandson Leon Gorman took over the business with sales of $3 million but a profit of only $70,000.

Gorman converted the mailing list from hand-typed to computers. He added credit cards in 1976 (now more than half their volume). Telephone orders are 25 percent of their sales. This means 2.6 million phone calls a year are handled by a staff of 430 telephone operators.

Gorman changed the catalog mailings from two a year to 10 a year. His reasoning: Why should we decide when the customer is ready to buy? Why not let the customer decide? And so, 60 million catalogs are mailed every year that result in annual mailings of 6 million packages.

Many items in the catalog do not pay their way but they remain because of what we call "Negative/Positive Merchandising." How-it-works: The customer, browsing through the catalog, sees the axes and tents and sleeping bags and clothing which takes on a different aura when tucked in with all this camp equipment. "We would not sell the casual clothing (positive) if we didn't have duck decoys (negative) in the book," says one of their senior officers.

What about tomorrow?

Some say it will be "electronic shopping."

Turn on your TV and dial-a-store or a product. Some retailers have even installed these TV monitors and order takers in their store, which could be the ultimate merging of both entities or the very first Chicken Omelette.

In Germany, the Bildschirmtext system is considered the most advanced interactive TV system used by a wide variety of catalog firms. But when asked about their success they simply answer, "Interesting developments."

In the United States, R.R. Donnelley has an Electronic Store division now being installed in 25 stores. You walk from a dark interior into a little cubby hole and you are in your own shopping environment.

"Compuserve" has nearly 150 advertisers on their interactive home shopping service and sells items ranging from Rolex watches to live lobsters to insurance. One major drawback to all these systems is the cost.

Consumers pay so many dollars per hour just to connect with the service. As quickly as someone say this is the way to go, someone else closes down.

A more exciting idea is the recent decision of the luxury automobile manufacturers (Porche and Mercedes) to send small videocassettes for customers to play on their TV and then order the merchandise. Expensive but effective.

Remember when we began this discussion by reminding you of the turn of the century with the threat of mail order? Listen to this quote from a store owner: "Catalogs are public enemy number one. They are a threat to the existence of retail stores. They are in existence to take customers out of your stores. We must band together to begin to formulate the kinds of strategies to insure our survival!"

That quote was not from the turn of the century. That was a recent statement from Donald Zale, chairman of Zale's jewelry chain that does more than $1 billion of business a year!

Perhaps the solution for Zale's jewelry store is the same solution decided on by other retailers we mentioned today. Try it. You'll probably like it.

Because if you want to make sure you have a chicken in every pot, don't put all your eggs in one basket.

How a Supermarket Increases Business Being The First To Contact TheNewly Married, Newly Arrived or Newly Born

20

If you are newly married, or moving to rural southwestern Wisconsin, the odds are you will food shop at Dick's supermarkets.

This seven store supermarket chain captures the major share of the retail food dollars in their market — with direct mail.

Their direct mail promotion began about 20 years ago, says President William Brodbeck, and is still going strong.

Here's how it works:

1. The Lists. Store personnel put together three lists daily:

The newly arrived: People who just moved into any shopping area with a Dick's supermarket. These names come from utilities, chambers of commerce, newspapers, and personal knowledge.

The newly married: Names culled from the society pages of the area newspapers.

The newly-born: From birth announcements.

2. The Letters. The first two groups receive a letter from the manager of their nearest Dick's supermarket. He welcomes them to the community. He tells about Dick's. He lists the benefits and special features of his store. He also gives the customer a special offer.

3. The Offer. Included with each letter are six different coupons. Each is good for one free food item. One coupon redeemable each week for six consecutive weeks.

The coupons are for the most wanted food items: a five pound bag of Idaho potatoes, a pound of cottage cheese, a dozen eggs, a half gallon of milk. All free.

4. The Next Letter. Bill Brodbeck, President of Dick's, writes a follow-up note about three weeks later, "Thanks for using the coupons." (How does he know they are used? He doesn't bother to check since 90% of all mailed coupons are redeemed!)

He asks this new buyer a favor. Since they are now customers of Dick's they can help the store do an even better job if they simply answer the questions in the enclosed questionnaire, with a stamped, self addressed envelope.

And, oh yes, for taking the time to answer the questionaire, Dick's has included for you **another** six free food coupons to use one a week for the next six weeks.

5. The Follow-Up. One year later this "new" customer has become a "steady" customer. Time for a new questionaire based on their experience with the store over the past year. A come-up file tells the secretary when the year has gone by. And for taking the time to answer the questions, Dick's has enclosed, for you, a coupon for free goods at their bakery department.

6. The Results: Customers feel they are part of the Dick's family. The communities are all small where Dick's stores are located (population varies from 2,400 to 9,500). Everyone knows everyone. And everyone knows, respects and simply likes to shop at Dick's.

Customers also see their comments on the questionnaires put into action. ("We get back more than 85% of the questionnaires we send out." says Brodbeck. "And we read each one of them for ideas and suggestions.")

One repeated suggestion was a preference for bulk produce instead of pre-packaged. (Translation: you can pick and choose and hold and feel and examine each apple, orange, grape, tomato, instead of having them pre-packaged and pre-selected and pre-priced by the store.) Dick's switched to what the customers wanted. Sales increased!

The other value of the questionnaire: cross-selling. When a customer is asked an opinion on the photo finishing or recipe cards services ("Do you pick up our recipe cards each week?"), some never knew, until that moment, the store had photo finishing and recipe cards. The questionnaire became a selling tool, a subconscious reminder, "If this is what you want to also buy, we have it, folks."

The third mailer is the most recent in their promotion. This letter goes to the newborn babies. The names are sent to Dick's by local hospitals. This letter is addressed to the baby by name with a $2.00 coupon for "your parents to use" for any baby product from food to clothing to accessories.

One year later, the baby receives another letter with congratulations on their birthday and, ah, yes, a coupon for 25 percent off their first birthday cake from the bakery department.

When asked what changes were made in the program in the decade since it began, Brodbeck answered, "very little." If Dick's opens a new department in a particular store, they add that information to the letter. But the copy has not changed. And the food items have not changed.

The original choice of giving away basic foods items is as strong a pull today as the day first mailing went out. "We wanted items with a universal appeal and the highest usage. What worked when we first tried it, Brodbeck says, still works today."

Remember: The letters, while not changing, are really new to the customer receiving them for the first time. To Dick's it is the same letter mailed a decade ago. To the person receiving the letter, it is as fresh, interesting and up-to-date as that morning's newspaper. (From which Dick's may have found their name).

Does Bill Brodbeck recommend this direct mail program for other food retailers? Yes! "It's an excellent way to encourage the customer to shop your store on multiple occasions. The value of the free coupons almost guarantees that will happen."

The trick of course is to catch the customer before they start a habit pattern by shopping a competitive store. He adds, "By attracting these new customers to our store early, we have a great opportunity to convince them our store is **the** store they ought to shop."

A few years ago, addressing Food Marketing Institute's national convention of thousands of retail food stores from all over the United States, Brodbeck talked about his store saying, "Our reputation rests on a very open relationship with our customers. We do our best to communicate with them often and in meaningful ways."

That basic philosophy is behind this very successful direct marketing campaign. "Above all," he sums up, "we must keep the lines of communication open with our customers."

This well-coordinated, thought-out and carefully-followed-through direct marketing program is a guide for any merchant in any business. It is also a reminder that the customer not only has to be originally sought, but he/she must also be continually looked after and listened to.

But if you move to Southwestern Wisconsin, you can be certain that upon your arrival, marriage, or birth of a child, your mail will soon contain a welcome letter from Dick's telling you who he is, what he does, why his store is in business, and a coupon invitation to come and visit and be part of the store's growing family.

21

Pack Up Your Troubles In Your Old K.I.T. Bag and Smile, Smile, Smile...

It was mid-1980, and sales were down. Interest rates were rising. Major chains were showing a loss for the first time in a decade.

Philadelphia Life Insurance Company had a meeting with its top performers, asking what could be done to increase business. Philosophies were exchanged. Concepts viewed. Formats reworked. Suddenly, Russel Gohn, from York, Pennsylvania, looked over the group and gave his solution: "It's nothing 2,000 sales calls won't cure..."

Russel Gohn was going after the new customer with the Fuller Brush technique — knock on enough doors, and you will make enough sales.

But, success is always available where it is least sought: with the customer you have.

And yes, American businesses spends five times as much on new customers as on the customers they already have.

Why?

Doen't make sense. The American Management Association says 65 percent of your customers are repeat customers. How can we have them repeat more often? That's our goal. Remember our fist two rules of selling:

Raphel Rule #1 — "Find out what your customer wants and give it to them.

Raphel Rule #2 — "Tis far, far easier to sell more to the customer you have than to sell to a new customer."

What we're saying, folks, is this: If you want your sales to increase, if you want your business to grow, if you want more ringings of your register, practice a proven, successful, and winning formula called Keep in Touch. which, for the purpose of this column, we condense to the initials K.I.T.

If you have a bank, and customers have a checking account, why don't they have a saving account? And if they have a checking and savings account, and an IRA, why not a loan? And if they have a checking and savings account, an IRA, and a loan, why not a . . .well, you get the idea.

If you have a supermarket you know your average customer spends about $80 a week with you. And, therefore (say you), they cannot spend anymore. Makes sense, **until** you see the same customer coming out of a nearby convenience store with **another** bag of groceries. These are not only the **same** groceries you have in your store, but groceries that cost more in the convenience store.

If you have a clothing store you know what your customers can afford to spend, based on their past experience with you, their job, and the size of their family. And you are content to have a good triple figure sale with a customer at the beginning of a season. You conclude they spent as much as they can afford. **Until** you see them come out of **another** store in the nearby shopping mall with **another** shopping bag full of clothing similar to what you sell in your store.

The ancient Roman philosopher Pareto was the first to tell us about the 80-20 rule. (Remember that one? Let's have a show of hands for those that remember. Good!) Pareto said 80 percent of your sales are brought to you by only 20 percent of your customers. Fund raisers for major political campaigns or charity drives say, "Yes, we want a lot of names to establish the bandwagon approach." ("Eveybody's contributing. Don't you want to be among the bunch?")

But their real effort, their intense drive, their pinpoint marketing is keyed to the much, much smaller group who (the 20 percent) wind up giving the lion's share of the money (the 80 percent).

Sometimes the figures are even more dramatic than that. Roger Horchow in his book, "Elephants In Your Mailbox" writes about his business in 1974 when "the rent payers were ten customers who were spending over $10,000 a year with us."

Competition gets tougher as new products, ideas, stores spring up around you. Remember if your business is good, it's because you are buying well and selling well. It's because you are doing something right.

And if business is bad, it's not the weather, It's not the economy. It's not the location, it's you. You are doing something wrong — because somebody is buying something somewhere! Your job is to figure out how to have customers spend a larger part of their disposable dollars in your store, buying **your** merchandise.

This philosophy is best practiced by a major association of meat packers. This association says that a stomach has only so much capacity — say 14 ounces. The goal of the meat packers to take up as many of these ounces as possible.

The goal of your business is to capture as many of those dollars as possible.

And you have the **K.I.T.** to do it.

The reason **K.I.T** works is that your customers want to hear from you. They shop your store. They spend their money with you. They trust you. Your letter in the mail, your voice over the phone is familiar, comfortable, easy. People like to do things from habit. Of course, there are the adventurers who want to vacation in a different city every year.

But there are far more who buy the second home or condominium in a familiar place because they are "comfortable" there. People are uncomfortable in a new place or strange surroundings. Everyone wants to be familiar, comfortable, at home.

And your customers feel that way in your place of business. If something happens with your business and they are not informed, they are resentful. It's like a friend telling secrets and leaving you out. You get mad. That is what happened to Roger Baily, a bank officer in Grand Island, Nebraska.

He writes: "We sent an extensive mailing to customers advertising our ATM (automatic teller machines). One was inadvertently sent empty — the addressed envelope but nothing inside. The customer called and asked what was in the envelope. After all, if it came from her bank it must be important.

"I apologized, explained the brochure and thought that ended the conversation. I was wrong. The customer insisted I send the brochure anyway. She wanted to see what she missed from her bank. . ."

If we send a mailing piece from our store about a sale or a new product and someone does not receive the package, we receive a phone call:

"I was just talking to my neighbors, and they told me they received this letter from you. Why didn't we receive one at our house?"

No explanation of post office delay, or mistake of the mailing house will satisfy these customers. Either they are a customer or they are not. "Will we please send them a copy of the advertisement at once."

We will, we will. . .

Now, when was the last time you received a phone call from a customer saying, "I haven't seen your ad in the newspaper for a couple of weeks, how come?" Or "I've been listening to the radio for the past few weeks and haven't heard any ads from you. How come?"

But, forget to include them on a store mailing and watch the phone jump off the hook. Or have them receive the mail after the promotion and be prepared for an onslaught of irate customers calling.

What all this proves is that your customers care. They want to know. They will respond to your calling or writing, your **K.I.T.**

And so when business is off and sales are down and you stare at the front doors wondering when the next customer will come in, start planning on what you will do today to let your present customer know they are there to be cherished, loved, and fussed-over.

Pick up a pen and paper write your customer a personal note about a sale or merchandise just-for-them. They will be impressed and will come to see you.

And you can pack up your troubles in your old K.I.T bag and smile, smile, smile.

22 The Pluck Of The Irish

The car in front of us on the road to Blarney, Ireland, was slowing down, speeding up, unsure where to make a turn when it came to a crossroad.

We pulled alongside and asked if we could help.

"Is this the road to Blarney?" asked the driver.

"Yes," we said, "Follow us. You must be on your way to Blarney Castle to kiss the Blarney Stone."

"No," he said, "I'm on my way to Blarney Woollen Mills to buy some sweaters."

Although the first reason for visiting this beautiful village in southeastern Ireland is still a castle built in the 10th century, the second reason is a business that began in 1980. "Blarney Woollen Mills. A family company."

The descriptive phrase "a family company" means what it says, for the Kelleher family — father, mother, seven children and in-laws — all run Blarney Woollen Mills.

THE COMPANY'S ROOTS go back to 1929 when the father, Christy Kelleher, went to work in Martin Mahony's Woollen Mills in Blarney. He remained there for 20 years working his way up to assistant supervisor.

In 1951 he left to sell insurance. But the feel of the cloth and the knowledge of the textiles never left him. In 1966, Kelleher opened his own shop, Blarney Handcrafts, located in a traditional Irish thatched cottage alongside historic Blarney Castle.

Kelleher's insistence on having only the very best quality led to the opening of his own small factory three years later where he could maintain control of the products. He made men's and women's knitwear for both local trade and export.

"Dad's goal was to always have the best," says daughter Freda, who buys for the retail shop. "He once had a grocery store. He found the one farmer whose produce was always superior. So he bought the farm."

Labor for Christy's new factory was supplied in part by his own household: wife Maureen and their seven children. Each of the sons and daughters became involved in different parts of his new and fast-growing business, starting when they were tall enough to reach the shelves and fold sweaters.

One morning in 1975, Christy heard the sad news that the Mahony wool mill was closing. Gone were 700 jobs. Sold was the machinery. Closed was the fine house. Silent the mill and red quarry stone building. Only the church remained to console the sad parishioners.

Christy Kelleher walked to the now-empty mill many days after work remembering his earlier two decades working there. His new business was rapidly growing. But was it growing fast enough to buy the mill where he once worked? Would the venture be too large? The costs too high? The expansion too soon?

On the other hand, his business was growing rapidly. His children were growing older and taking an active interest. He would gain not only room to grow but also control over the quality of his product.

So he bought the mill. He moved his small knit-wear factory to the big mill where it fitted comfortably on just the top floor. The ground floor which Christy had known as the "combing department" for the unravelling of the wool yarn, now became a retail shop of gifts and crafts. The Victorian house was tastefully renovated to retain the original character and charm. Today it is a 10-bedroom hotel named "Christy's" (after you know who).

Each of his children has a specific responsibility — seven buyers for seven businesses.

Marian Kelleher O'Gorman is buyer for the retail shop.

Frank Kelleher runs the hotel.

Pat Kelleher handles the shipment of merchandise.

Pascal runs the knitwear factory.

Kevin is in charge of the wholesale division.

Bernadette takes care of the Blarney Woollen Mills shop in downtown Dublin.

And daughter Freda works with Marian buying for the retail shop. She also skitters about with her father's enthusiasm, now helping with a sale, now taking stock, now greeting people in the shop. An Irish jig on fast forward.

One night Marian came home to husband Michael complaining of too much work. Would Michael come into the business? Yes. He left his rental van business and handles the rapidly growing mail order division.

The children are so busy they cannot handle the normal, everyday chores young people are supposed to handle. When it's time to pick up **their** children from school, Christy is the one chosen. "The children are too busy in the business," explains the proud grandfather.

Their enthusiasm and excitement is contagious and everyone in the shop is helpful, kind, courteous — all the Boy Scout adjectives. It begins when the sales force walks into work in the morning. There, at the entrance, is a big sign that says it all: "The customer is **always** right!"

The main floor store department caters to busloads of tourists who are among the **quarter million** customers that visit Blarney. As buses stop, visitors are first greeted by Christy himself. He climbs aboard the bus and welcomes them with the traditional Irish greeting "Cead Mile Failte" ("A 100,000 welcomes") to his home, his business, his own little "castle" in Blarney.

Then the tourists and visitors leave the buses and shop for pure, hand-knit Aran sweaters (named after the small islands off the Irish coast where the wool is strong and sturdy). They choose from tweed coats and suits, mohair shawls, Avoca hand-woven bedspreads, Waterford and Cavan crystal, Irish Dresden, Royal doulton figurines and tableware, Hummel figurines, Belleek china, Celtic jewelry, Swarovski silver crystal. . .

The store is open seven days a week year-round from 9 a.m. to 5:30 p.m. (with later hours Monday to Friday from May through September).

And when you leave the retail shop, one of the family is there to thank you for coming, don't forget to come back and "Slan Dia dhiu" — "Goodbye. And God be with you."

Many customers pick and choose their gifts and ask to have them mailed. The Blarney team is glad to oblige. One day Michael looked at the list of names that totaled nearly 100,000 (90 percent Americans) and realized he had a strong database. Could this be the beginnings of Blarney Mill mail order business?

Yes! He put the names and addresses on computers and in 1985 he put together a list most wanted items for his first Christmas catalog.

Response was strong enough to set up a separate mail order company.

What is the future for Blarney Mills?

More busloads of tourists. More names on the mailing list. More mail order to America.(For their next catalog Write to Michael O'Gorman at Blarney Woollen Mills, County Cork, Ireland.) After all, there's 3 1/2 million Irish in Ireland. But more than 40 million of Irish descent in America!

The mail order division of Blarney Woollen Mills is like the Irish direct mail industry: New, exciting and chock-full of interest.

They know the future is great for their business — "Blarney Woollen Mills — A family business." With only one caveat: As Michael says, "The day we forget we're a family is the day we will not be successful."

23

How A Cut-up
Inspired Successful
DM

This is about a famous French artist — and how his creative legacy was responsible for dramatic results in direct mail.

The story begins with the *Livs* (translation: Food) supermarket tucked downstairs inside the quality NK department store in Stockholm.

The idea of having an area with built-in traffic appeals to supermarketeers. They worked on cooperative leasing/renting/merchandising going back to the early 1950s with large department stores throughout Europe.

The reason it works: Retailers who operate leased departments know success is achieved when there is a compatibility of like-quality merchants. Putting a fast-food operation next to a sophisticated fur shop is not to be desired in terms of merchandising mix. It confuses the customer.

This meant that *Livs*, like the NK store in which it is housed, had to be upscale, quality, prestigious. And it is. No sugar and spice in this store, but everything nice. No milk or bread basics, but 100 varieties of tea and 200 varieties of just **dessert** cheese. The Queen of Sweden shops here (by herself) and customers pay for parking.

How do you advertise this upscale store? Not the traditional jam-packed, 1,000-items-to-the-page listings as found in most supermarket ads. The advertising for this supermarket had to have the same quality look as the NK store.

How, wondered manager Thore Wernold, could this be done?

It was an art exhibit featuring the famed "cutouts" by artist Henri Matisse that gave him the idea. The exhibit had just closed in Stockholm. More than 600,000 Swedes came to this exhibit! That meant nearly one out of every 10 people in Sweden saw this art show.

Now, was there a way Wernolf could tie in with Matisse. . . and transfer the characteristics of the artist to that of the store?

Wernolf contacted his advertising agency. Could they put together an advertising campaign for his food store that would look as though it had the feeling of Matisse?

They did. Soon, full-page ads appeared in the Stockholm daily newspapers with a close resemblance to the famed Matisse "cut-outs." Simple splashes of colors with a phrase or two ("Supper for two?") and the logo of the store.

Reaction? "People immediately associated Matisse with our store," said Wernolf. The style of the painter Matisse became the style of the supermarket.

The ads were so successful, people asked for copies to frame and put in their homes.

Now, if it worked as a newspaper ad to tell people about Livs, could it also work as a direct mail piece to tell customers what the store sold? And have them come and buy? Why not try?

Within a few blocks of the NK department store are the headquarters of 90 percent of all the large Swedish companies. Wernolf sent them a mailer asking if they would like to have a coupon booklet offering specials on successive weeks. The illustration in the booklet were put together to look like — you guessed it — Matisse "cutouts."

More than 35,000 individuals working in these companies received the letter and more than 8,000 said, "Send the booklets!" The store did, and immediately saw a jump in volume from their neighbors who, until they received the mailer, never thought of buying groceries in the area where they worked.

The campaign continued with more brochures, booklets, coupons, recipe cards, all with a Matisse "look" — and all bringing customers to this supermarket in the NK department store in Stockholm.

How successful was all this?

This successful: Every year there is a contest run in Swedish magazines to pick the "most recognizable" advertisement run during the year. Last year's winner, identified by 86 percent of the customers, was *Liv's* "Matisse" ads.

24 What This Country Needs Is A Good Five Senses

As vice president of the United States under Woodrow Wilson, Thomas Riley Marshall was presiding over the U. S. Senate. Once, when he was listening to a rather tedious debate on the needs of the country, he leaned over to John Crockett, chief clerk of the U. S. Senate, and said, "What this country needs is a good five cent cigar." *

We've thought about that and came to the conclusion that what an effective retail direct mail piece needs is a good five **senses**. Touch, taste, hear, smell and sight. One, all, or any combination will contribute to the success of your next mailing.

TOUCH: Menswear retailers tell us when they include an actual swatch of fabric in their mailings, sales increase dramatically. There is a company in Germany that sends a catalog of women's clothing. Each page has a swatch of the actual fabric. The catalogs cost the sender $5 apiece or more. But the results are worth it. (They do ask the receivers of the catalog if they do NOT buy, to send it back postage pre-paid. The catalogs are simply too expensive.) But their niche in marketing and their success in sales

* To which Franklin Adams, years later added, "What this country needs is a good five cent nickel."

is because the consumer can actually touch the fabric. The feel of cashmere, silk or pure cotton simply accomplishes one basic goal: increased sales.

TASTE: How do manufacturers make the consumer purchase their product? By sending test samples through the mail. And so minipackages of breakfast cereal, tiny tubes of toothpaste, a weekend supply of hand lotion are all sent. Other manufacturers know the quickest way to have you buy their product is to have you taste it. Supermarkets do this all the time with sample tasting areas set up for you to try the latest pizza, cheese soup. and every time (make that EVERY time), manufacturers run these tasting demonstrations, sales of the product double, triple or more.

HEAR: For many years, Eva-Tone made paper-thin plastic records to be sent to customers who could listen to a manufacturer's message on their home record players. They advertised everything from radio commercials to encyclopedias. Audiocassttes can now be used in a similar fashion.

And who among you are old enough to remember the narrow pieces of plastic you dragged through a hole in the cardboard that would "say" the name of the product?

And so "sound," meaning the ability to **hear** the selling message, is another "sense" of selling.

SMELL: We are all familiar with 3M's "scratch and sniff" program. 3M capsules the aroma of specific product into a small area on a mailing piece. A simple scratching of this section releases the actual aroma.

One you have seen: The department store statements that feature perfume enclosure ads.

Our favorite story: Save-Mor supermarkets in Tennessee found a company that made ink to match any odor. Save-Mor thought this was a good way to promote its produce. The store ran ads saying, "Bananas so delicious you can actually smell them." And you could, By simply holding the paper close to your nose you inhaled the scent of bananas. The scent remained for about 12 hours. The next week, strawberries. The next week, lemons. The last promotion was oranges, But the night before the ad ran, the ad manager of Save-Mor was called by a production man from the newspaper.

"The orange scent hasn't arrived from the chemical plant," he said, "You have two choices. Either run the ad without the smell or run a blank page." The ad manager hesitated, then reluctantly said, "Run the ad without the smell. . . " And the ad ran with the headline, "Oranges so delicious you can actually smell them."

And all week people went into the store and said, "Y'know you finally got the smell right. Now THAT was oranges!"

SIGHT: Today's businesses find their competition staring at them from cable stations all over the United States. Suddenly, billions of dollars for products and services are spent by sight. You watch the TV, pick up the phone and order the merchandise. Whether it is J.C. Penney, Sears, the Home Shopping Network, QVC or any of the other imitations — all of them come into the home of the retailer's customer offering their product by actual sight.

What is selling by "sight"? Jewelry is high on the list. Hard goods and stereos sell well. Clothing is more difficult because it involves fit and people want to feel it (another one of the "sensible" reasons).

But since most businesses deal only in words through letters, mailers and statement enclosures, they wonder if it makes sense to use **one** sense. The answer: YES, because words alone are capable of expressing ALL the senses. Here's how:

TOUCH: If you tell you reader the cloth is smooth as silk, the beard rough as sandpaper, they immediately perceive the sense of touch.

TASTE: Ask your reader to imagine sucking on a lemon and their lips will purse. Tell them to visualize Thanksgiving turkey with the slightly crisp baked meat, the tender vegetables, the whipped creamy potatoes. . . and they sense the taste.

HEAR: You can talk to your reader in a whisper as low as this or a scream as **LOUD AS THIS!**

SMELL: Talk about the odor of chestnuts roasting, the scent of just-baked apple pie out of the oven, the strong scent of garlic, the sense of smell is captured.

SIGHT: The art of seeing is the art of reading. Remember that in the beginning there was. . . the word.

So the next time you put together the direct mailer for your store, ask yourself "Does it make any senses? Which of the five does it use?" The more you use, the greater your chances for success.

And when it works. . . well, congratulations. Have a cigar!

25

How A "Down Under" Promotion Came Out On Top

The setting is a fine restaurant in Australia. You and your guest have just finished dining. The waiter brings you the check. You hand him you credit card and another shiny black card with gold lettering. The waiter takes back the check and subtracts the cost of one of the main entrees.

The setting changes. You check into a fine hotel. The front desk clerk quotes you the rate for your room. Again, you pull out the shiny black card with the gold lettering. He quickly corrects his quoted price and offers you the same room at a savings of 20 to 50 percent.

The setting changes. You are at a movie theater, buying tickets for two. You present the card and receive two tickets for the price of one. Or . . . you rent a car, show the card, receive a discount.

What is this "magic" card that saves you money everytime you use it? This one: The Presidential Card.

Nearly 100,000 Australians are members. They pay $69 a year for the privilege of having this money-saving plastic in the pocket (or pocketbook). They join (and rejoin) because of an ongoing, effective, results-producing direct mail campaign.

The Presidential Card is owned and operated by Tony Ingleton in Melbourne. Card members are located throughout Australia. They use their card in more than 500 Australian establishments.

The card is really an adaptation of the "twofer" coupons we see appear once and again in many American cities which, in turn, are a variation of the "buy one, get one free" coupon booklets often sponsored by local charitable groups. What makes the Presidential Card different is that it is just that: a card. It tucks in your wallet with your American Express, Diners, Visa, or Master Charge card. Take out one to pay your bill, add the Presidential Card and presto, the bill is changed to a lower amount.

It all began in 1964. Dan Richard, an American from Beach Haven Crest, New Jersey, came to Australia and put together a dine-around coupon booklet similar to programs he ran successfully in the U.S. He convinced about 15 restaurants in Melbourne to participate. If their customers bought one meal, they could have another meal. . . free.

The restaurants agreed because it brought in more customers. If they sold a few drinks or an extra dessert, a potential loss quickly became a found profit.

One of the restaurants in the program was owned by Tony Ingleton's father, John. He saw the growing success of this idea and decided to go into business for himself. He expanded the concept throughout Australia.

In 1980, father and son came up with the idea of having one card instead of many paper coupons. The card could be used over and over again — even in the same restaurant.

To attract the better-known restaurants, he changed the rules. No longer would the restaurant give the second **meal** free — they would give the second **main course** free. Now the restaurant could actually make a good profit from the sale of the appetizer and/or soup and/or salad and/or dessert.

The upgrading of the image required an upgrading of the name which at that time had a different title in every city. The presidency of a corporation connotes a strong image of special service. Ergo, why not call the program "Presidential." And since it involved a card, why not the "Presidential Card?"

The acceptance of this new card called for expansion — not just in every Australian state and major city but also in services. If a restaurant with many empty tables would offer discounts to bring in traffic, could a hotel with many empty rooms offer discounts to bring in traffic? (Answer: Yes!) And so would car rental firms. And movies. And tourist parks. . .

The Presidential Card grew rapidly. Tony's father left to raise horses and Tony took over. He traveled throughout Australia drumming up business, extolling the card, convincing establishments they had nothing to lose and customers to gain. His personality and belief in the product convinced even the original doubters. Soon his phone began ringing with restaurants and hotels calling him and asking to be listed in his directory.

The Presidential Card prides itself on high standards. The "look" is important because it projects an "image" — not just to the service establishment but also (and even more important) to the cardholder.

How does anyone find out about the Presidential Card and what it has to offer?

Two ways: Space advertising and mailings to affinity groups.

How does the Presidential Card keep its members? One way: direct mail.

"Direct mail is the most cost-efficient way to put my message across and to establish the fact the Presidential Card is different from other types of discount operations," says Ingleton.

Here's how his direct mail program works:

• **Renewals:** When a customer's one year membership expires, they receive a letter **with their new card** telling all the changes and additions taking place plus an invoice for the new dues. More than 50 percent renew.

• **Non-renewals:** A follow-up letter goes out a month later reminding them to renew giving reasons why and advantages for Presidential Card members.

• **Affinity Groups:** The best response. People who belong to a social group or other common interest organization. The mailer is directed specifically to them, offering a lower price for their group. The affinity program resulted in his membership growing from 25,000 to 100,000 card holders in just two years! And having 100,000 members is Australia is like having two million in the U.S.

Ingleton mails nearly one million pieces a year either as separate letters or as inserts in Diners Club's *Signature* magazine, Australian Post's literature, Victorian Railways brochures to their members and other affinity groups.

Those who join promptly receive their black and gold presidential Card with their embossed name and a hefty 500 page impressive four color directory of service establishments.

A supplementary directory is mailed in June to the membership listing new places to visit, stay, dine (or those no longer in the program).

He recently experimented with a letter to ex-members — out of the program for a year or more — offering a transistor radio premium for rejoining. Picked up more than 200 renewals.

"I keep on finding new ways to use direct mail," he says citing his successful **Member Get a Member** program ("Sign up two new members and your next year's membership is free!")

He is experimenting with new letters, offering special premiums, thinking about setting up a special catalog of gifts for Presidential Card members ("If American Express can do it, why can't I?")

Today his staff of seven in Australia's key cities handle customer complaints and seek new business, always keeping in mind the quality standards Ingleton believes is essential to his success.

He believes the secret is caring about the customer. That's why he believes in direct mail. "It's the closest thing to actually sitting down with the customer in their living room."

And the total identification with the Presidential Card IS personal. Tony's smiling face is on the stationary and in each ad. His copy is first person, me-to-you and his brochure is chockfull of testimonials from customers who write him to say how much money they saved during the year using the card.

His sincerity and belief in his product leaps out from the copy. Right to the guarantee. Not just the traditional, "Try us for 30 days and your money back if your not satisfied." Yes, he does that. And more. His Added Value Extra Guarantee says if any card member goes to any establishment listed in the directory and, for any reason, does not receive the full credit allowed , simply write and tell him with a copy of the ad. He will send a check for the money that should have been saved.

"That's what I would want someone to do for me," he says. "So doesn't it make sense I should do that for card members?"

Sure. Which simply goes to prove it takes a man from down under to come out on top.

26

It's Consumer Wants, Not Needs, That Really Count.

The man who invented the vacuum cleaner went bankrupt. He sold the patents to a Mr. Hoover who bought this new-fangled electric broom to department store buyers. They turned it down. Their reason: There was no need for this contraption. Women bought brooms to clean floors and rugs. A broom did the job. It was not expensive. Who would want to spend more money for an electrical gadget that did the same job?

Hoover hired a salesforce that went door-to-door. They walked into living rooms all over America spilling dirt on rugs and them whisking them clean with this new "vacuum cleaner."

Gradually, every home had to have one. Gradually the department store began to stock them because the customer wanted this new cleaner.

What happened? A "want" was created by a clever marketing person.

Those in direct marketing who claim they are putting out products to fill their customers "needs" are living in the wrong century. We have not been a "needy" country for more than 50 years. Today's successful retailers, salespeople, direct mail firms are not need-fillers. They are want-creators.

As little children we are asked by adults, "What do you want to be when you grow up?" No one says, "What do you need to be?" The reason is simple. If you "want" something strong enough you will produce it, work for it or buy it.

The United States Government updates an inventory of necessities for people on welfare. At one time this list included only shelter, food and basic clothing. Today, it includes basic kitchen appliances. And a television set. The "wants" have become the "needs."

Our job, as business people, is to create **wants.**

The promotion, advertising, marketing of a product is the first part. The quality and integrity and results are the second part. Both must be present to be successful. Otherwise you have the reaction of the Maypo breakfast cereal TV commercial.

A little child cries, "I want my Maypo." Parents throughout the country buy the breakfast cereal and take it home. But the children did not eat it. They did not like the maple taste. Good marketing. Bad results. The old theory, you can bring a horse to water, but you can't make him drink.

Here's some other examples of transferring "wants" to "needs."

• The jean market is owned by Lee, Levis, and Wrangler, popular priced jeans worn by all ages. Suddenly Diane Von Furstenberg creates a new product: designer jeans. This new skin-tight fashion jean is shown, modeled with fur coats and dinner jackets. Jeans similar to the time-honored styles only in content of fabric but not in shape or fit.

Was there a "need" for a pair of blue jeans that sold for two or three times the price of "regular" jeans? No. Did people buy them? Yes. Was a whole new market of "designer" jeans created? Yes, to the point where Levis, seeking to increase their market, now sells J.C. Penney's and Sears. The traditional retailers, the major department stores, cut back on Levis inventory to "position" themselves separate and apart from catalog and/or discount stores, and carry "designer" jeans.

• Joe Sugarman's electronic wizardry catalog is a good example of creating "wants." To the point where he now accepts orders for portable telephones on planes. No price yet. Hasn't figured out the cost. But if you'd like to reserve one, he's willing. Is there a "need" for a portable telephone to call someone when you're 35,000 miles straight up? Joe thinks he can create a want. And a few years from now, people will think this phone was always available for a few dollars extra charge along with a headset to watch the movies.

• L.L. Bean's catalog business jumped when their merchandise was suddenly "discovered" by people across the United States as something they "wanted." Suddenly the company receives the prestigious Coty award for "outstanding design." Leon Gorman, grandson of the founder, wonders why he wins awards for the same merchandise they have been selling for half a century? Simple answer: the product originally conceived as a "need". . . became a "want."

Then there are repositioned "wants. . . "

• Vrest Orton founded the "Voice of the Mountains" Vermont country Store catalog in Weston, Vermont, chock-full of merchandise originally available in stores only at the turn of the century. The soap-savers and corn-holder which were **yesterday's** "needs" have become **today's** "wants."

Some "wants" are short-lived fads. Others become long-term staples.

Fads include hula hoops, Nehru shirts, and, eventually, E. T.

Staples include record players (now it's CD's instead of 78's) computers and, consistently, Mickey Mouse.

The trick is to realize the world is changing, and the typewriter staple was first mechanical, then electrical and now computerable.

The world of human knowledge now doubles almost every 24 months. You realize this when some tells you (fact) that 93 percent of all scientists that ever lived are alive today.

But if someone told you 10 years ago one out of four automobiles sold in the United States would be made in Japan, would you have believed them?

And if someone told you Harley Davidson, who was making 85 out 100 motorcycles in the U.S. in the late 1950's now makes less than one out of 100, would you have believed them?

Or, if someone told you ten years ago a $12,000 hand-held computer would be available today for about $5, would you have believe them?

Probably not.

It would be difficult to believe (1) such a drastic change would take place and (2) it was brought about by a switch in the consumer "wants."

What all this proves to all of us in our businesses, our selling, our direct mail, is that the road to success is always under construction. That what has been bears little relationship to what is and less to what will be. That successful business people (like successful doctors, lawyers, accountants) remain successful only by being aware of what is going on around them.

A recent survey said Americans spent nearly $500 per person last year on hair conditioners, shampoos and trips to barbers or beauty parlors. The question is: If you spend that much on the outside of your head, how much do you spend on the **inside** of your head?

Do you watch, observe, read listen to what is happening in your business? Do you set aside time to study, reflect and plan about where you will be tomorrow? Are you so caught up in day-to-day activity that you wake up one morning and wonder when it happened that the world passed you by?

Set aside time from your schedule to simply observe. . . and think.

Not because you need to.

Because you want to.

Part Three

Making The Sale

27

Ten Characteristics
of Top
Salesmen!

*Willy: Ben. I've been waiting for you for so long! What's the
answer? How did you do it?*
Ben: Oh, there's a story in that. . .
                    —Death of a Salesman

Willy Loman never did discover the story that made his
brother Ben successful. He knew Ben was successful. But why?

What makes a good salesman?

What makes some succeed and others fail?

Is there a guide, a list, a definition that will work for others to
see and follow and copy and learn and, in turn,. . . succeed?

This was the question facing author Edwin P. Hoyt.

His thinking: nothing happens until a sale is made. So how do
you make a sale?

He examined successful sales people throughout the country.
Did interviews. Queried the seller and the buyer.

Soon he discovered certain techniques and characteristics
repeated by the most successful people in selling.

He found he was able to narrow this list to ten. He published
them in his book, "America's Top Salesmen."

We present the list of ten to you with stories and examples to
read, think about and apply in your next business venture.

1. Work Hard. Promoter Bill Veeck who shattered the traditions of baseball when he owned the St. Louis Browns, Cleveland Indians, and the Chicago White Sox, once said, "I've met a lot of people that are smarter than I am, but I never met anyone that worked harder. . . "

You may remember the Rule of Three explained in a previous chapter. Here's how it works for the world's leading life insurance salesman, Ben Feldman. His first rule: "Work hard," Number two "Think Big," and Number three, "Listen very well." Complains Ben, "There's never enough time."

It also means **enjoying** your work. Vrest Orton who created the original Vermont Country Store in Weston, Vermont, said he couldn't wait to get up in the morning to go to work and "It never ceases to amaze me that people pay me money for what I enjoy doing so much." If you still don't have his catalog send 50 cents right now for some of the best direct mail copy written in catalogs today. Write his son Lyman, who now runs the business after his father/philosopher died, at Vermont Country Store, Weston, Vermont 05161. Ask for his most recent issue of "The Voice of the Mountains." (Tell him Murray sent you. . .)

Those that succeed in selling do not procrastinate. They do not seek reasons for not working. They work because they enjoy working. There is an old Chinese proverb, "He who cannot smile should not own a shop."

2. Self-Confident. Good salespeople have confidence in their ability to perform. This expresses itself in how they talk or how they write. The most effective direct mail copy is chock-full of facts and information expressing confidence on the part of the writer which then communicates itself to the reader. Dr. David Merrill says self confidence is "the degree to which you and I will go to sell ourselves and our ideas."

One way to increase this degree is by testing. American Express and other giant mail order catalog people first test their products in a small market. If it succeeds they then have the self confidence to mail the item to their total market.

Joe Girard, America's Number One Salesman (look it up in the Guinness Book of Records) said his secret is simply telling his customers they are not buying a car. "You buy me!" says Joe Girard. The customer doesn't have to worry about their car any more because Joe worries for them. Joe's confidence makes his customer believe.

The self confident person asks more. Expects more. And. . . gets more. The ancient Hindus said, "As one thinks, so one becomes. . . "

3. Self Discipline. The Unysis company advertises they conduct "listening" courses for their salespeople. They know our basic rule of selling: Find out what the customer wants. And give it to them! But you cannot do that if you keep on talking all the time. Or write voluminous copy that does not help sell your merchandise (if you do that, you're guilty of "listening to" what you have written rather than what the customer wants.) How many salespeople wait for the customer to finish what they are saying so **they** can say what they want to say **without having heard what the customer said!**

There is a certain discipline that goes with "listening." Famed advertising expert David Ogilvy advises young people who want to learn his profession, "Work for someone from whom you can gain an education. It is far more important when you are young to learn rather than earn."

An ancient Arabic proverb explains this concept: "If I listen, I have the advantage. If I speak, others have it."

And so it is when writing good advertising copy. There must be a compactness of words. You must tell the story simply, easily and well. You must not overstate the fact. It is easy to fall into the exaggeration trap. When this threatens remember Hamlet's advice to the players, "In the very whirlwind of your passion, you must acquire and begat a temperance that will give it smoothness." Understatement makes a product sound/ read/ become more believable to the viewer/ reader/ consumer. . .

Alan Laiken writes in his book, *How To Get Control of Your Time and Life*, about the importance of discipline in running your daily life. He suggests you compile a "To Do" list as you start each day. Check off each item as you complete it.

He instructs his readers to "Never handle a piece of paper more than once." Most people are paper pushers. They shove the mail from one corner of the desk to another. Laiken suggest dividing the mail into three piles: An "A" Pile (the most important) and a "B" pile (the not-as-important) and a "C" pile (the least important.) He then says you throw the "C" pile into the trash. This leaves an "A" pile and a "B" pile. Take the "B" pile and break it into an "A" pile and a "C" pile. Throw the "C" pile away. Now you only have an "A" pile.

Take this "A" pile and break it down by 1-2-3 priorities. Tackle them in their order of importance. Do **not** jump to one of the easier ones further down the list. Take them in order.

That's self discipline!

Avoid the trap of becoming so busy doing the inconsequential things you never do the things of consequence. .

You cannot sell your goods unless you list all the "A" steps from selection to choice of merchandise to testing to inventory to color vs. black and white fulfillment to credit and well. . . the idea is to practice discipline in organizing what has to be done. Then give each item priority number. And then work them out one-by-one.

4. Perseverance. Rare is the business that proves a financial success the first season. There is reputation to be built and confidence to be gained. There must be a steady ongoing consistency with a plan for the future: next month's campaign, nest year's catalog.

It is easy to give up. But to persevere is to use the knowledge you have gained from each proceeding campaign to increase the potential success of your next campaign.

A salesman used to call on us with merchandise we felt was not right for our store. After a few seasons we asked him how long he was going to call since we consistently turned down his lines.

"Well," He said. "It depends on which one of us dies first. . ."

McGraw-Hill surveys say it takes five repeat calls from a salesman to get an order from a client. How many salespeople quit after the first turn-down? Or the second? Or the third? The one that keeps plugging away and coming back will eventually write the sale. Fact: 20% of the salesmen sell 80% of the products.

Joe Girard (remember him a few paragraphs back?) knows once he completes a sale it is not the end but really the beginning. The customer becomes a prospect for (a) a second car (b) a new car two years or sooner down the road and (c) A recommendation to other customers for him to sell.

Every month Joe sends out 14,000 cards to his customers (add up **that** postage!) In January it's "Happy New Year. I like you. Joe Girard, Merollis Chevrolet." In February, it's "Happy Valentine's Day. I like you. Joe Girard, Merollis Chevrolet." In March, it's "Happy St. Patrick's Day. I like you. Joe Girard, Merollis Chevrolet."

A card every month. Look it up on your calender. There's **some** holiday every month. and an extra card on your birthday. "This is your special day. I like you. Joe Girard, Merollis Chevrolet."

Now, all together folks, whom do you call when it's time to buy a new or used car for your family? Why from the fellow who keeps on reminding you he likes you. From the man who makes a direct sale through his indirect use of direct mail. From the one who perserveres — Joe Girard.

For those who say, "Well good for Joe, but I tried and finally gave up," remind them Grandma Moses was still painting when she was 100 years old, George Bernard Shaw was still writing at 93, Eamon de Valera was President of Ireland at 91. Pablo Picasso still sketched at 90 and Michelangelo did architectural plans for the Church of Santa Maria degli Angeli when he was 90. (Maybe life begins at 90!)

5. Flexibility. (Or: Expectations vs. Realities). We can have the game plan all carefully worked out in our mind, but when the time comes to put it in action. . . it doesn't work. In fact, we can see it not working as we go along. Solution: Change the plan.

This **does not** mean to stop dreaming, planning, thinking. Those are your Expectations And you **must** continue with them throughout your life. For to think only of the Realities of Life is to give up without trying.

Consider the case of the man who failed in business and decided to run for political office as a state legislator. He ran, got beat and figured well, he really **was** a businessman so he went back into business. And failed the second time around. Back to politics. . . and finally made it to the State legislature. But was defeated when he tried to be Speaker of the House. And again, when he tried to be a presidential elector.

He ran for Congress and made it. Only to lose on the re-run. A few years later he tried to the U.S. Senate. . . and lost again. Two years later, he again tried for the U.S. Senate and, ah, yes, again he lost.

You can see he was building a no-win habit pattern faced with the re-occurring Realities of losing.

But his Expectations continued high. After this last defeat, he ran again, only two years later. . . and became President of the United States.

His name: Abraham Lincoln.

6. Goals other than money. When entertainer Merv Griffin had a talk show, he once interviewed "new" millionaires. Those who made it by themselves. He asked the question, "I guess one of your driving forces was to make a lot of money?"

In the silence that followed there was a negative shaking of heads. One by one they explained making money was simply the result. . . not the goal. One said there was the challenge to make a jet plane for an individual instead of just for airline companies. Another spoke of perfecting a food recipe and selling it to the mass market. Each in turn said they "had this idea," believed in it and worked for it. The motivation was the **challenge.** Money just happened. . .

Community involvement is another prime motive for success. Inherited wealth carries responsibility to the community that created the wealth — a philosophy handed down generation to generation by the Rockefellers, the Mellons, the Fords, and their respective and well-known foundations.

Each of us in business have an obligation over, above and beyond the simple exchange of goods for a price. We owe the community responsible for our success something in return: Part of the talent, knowledge or expertise we possess. Not simply writing a check. Anyone can do that. It means committing yourself to some degree. The reasons are not necessarily altruistic. For a healthier and wealthier community means more people are able to shop and buy the products and services you have for sale.

Try Giving Yourself Away is a book by David Dunn. His philosophy is simply that you gain in profession, your philosophy or your general well-being by simply giving of yourself to others.

Famed newscaster Bernard Meltzer tells of the time he was trying to raise money to go to college. Though accepted by tuition-free CCNY in New York City, he needed $100 for books. He approached a friend of the family he called Uncle Joe. He told him of the problem. Uncle Joe handed him a check for $100. Meltzer, overwhelmed said, "I don't know when I can pay you back the money. . ."

Uncle Joe replied: "You can never give me back the money, Bernard. I will not accept it. However there will come a time in the future when you will be successful. And someone will come to you for help. You must leave your door open and you must listen, and you must try to be of assistance. And then you can say, 'I'm paying back Uncle Joe. . .'"

7. Respect for the buyer's good sense. The con man making a living from hit-and-run will never succeed. His triumphs are of the moment, his success illusory. Only when you know, understand, and appreciate the problem of the customer will you develop the answer to their needs. Remember the basic of selling: **Find out what your customers want. And give it to them.**

Too often we do not practice the **Art of Active Listening.** We are all so wound-up, ready and eager to give our rehearsed and memorized selling presentation we are not listening to what the customer has to say.

We once went with a local real estate consultant to a bank officer for a real estate loan. Our meeting lasted less than five minutes and we received immediate approval.

"What happened," we asked in the hallway after the meeting. "Why did he say 'yes' so quickly?"

The learned, older real estate man looked at us and slowly said, "I never ask a question unless I know the answer is yes."

He assembled all the critical and necessary information. He summarized it quickly and presented the total package within a few minutes. The loan officer found all the necessary documentation he needed without having to give long explanations and detailed questioning. He gave his approval.

Our consultant simply knew what the customer wanted. . . and gave it to him. And the sale was made.

8. Willingness to learn from others. The intelligent person is the one who says, "I don't know" when asked a question for which they do not know the answer. When they quickly add, "But I'll find out and get right back to you," they are simply willing to learn from others."

We often fall into the "Curse of Assumption." We know what we do, when we do it, where we do it, so we assume everyone else also knows.

Not true.

My father used to sell insurance for Metropolitan Life Insurance Company. It was the time of the depression. He collected a quarter a week premium from customers. One day he told a customer, "Instead of coming to the door every week, simply leave two quarters in an envelope with your receipt book in your mailbox."

She agreed. He did this for six months. One week he opened the mailbox and saw his envelope with the two quarters. And another from the Prudential Insurance Company with another quarter.

He rang the bell. The customer answered the door. "Tell me," he asked her, "Are you mad at me?"

"Why no," she explained, "Why would you think so?"

He explained he collected her premium every week for six months. Today he saw another insurance policy — written by his competition.

The woman looked surprised and said, "Oh. Do you **sell** insurance? I thought you were just a collector."

"Curse of Assumption."

From that moment on, my father always told his customers he was a life insurance **salesman.**

9. Ability to handle big money. "I never think in dollars when I buy," said an experienced clothes buyer the other day. "I know my budget. I am conscious of units. But if I start relating my 'buying' dollars to the dollars in my pocketbook, I would be destroyed, lose my confidence, and run screaming for the room."

She's right.

People who handle big money use it as a tool as a carpenter uses his tools or a chemist uses his tools. Money merely becomes a medium of exchange.

Of course, this implies you have a knowledge of your product, your market and confidence in what you are buying.

Story: James Cooper, an attorney, community leader, businessman, and successful fund-raiser in Atlantic City, New Jersey, chaired a meeting of a non-profit foundation one day. The group was discussing a new project and one member said, "That's too much money. We can't do that." Cooper quickly answered , "Let's decide what we want to do. Then we'll figure out how to get the money."

His thinking: Don't let the big dollars scare you. If you have a goal. And a desire. And a plan. You can make it happen. . .

10. Perfectionist. President Jimmy Carter tells of the time he was a captain in the navy and reported to his superior, Admiral Hyman Rickover, after completing an assigned task.

"I have completed the job," said Carter.

Rickover looked up from his desk, and quietly said, "Is it the very best you could do?"

"Pardon, sir?" said Carter not quite sure what the admiral meant.

"Did you do the very best you could possibly do on that job?" said Rickover.

Carter hesitated and then said, "I'll check it out, sir, and report back."

Rickover demanded perfection. Carter checked it out, came back, saluted and said, "The job is finished sir." Rickover didn't even look up as he said, "Dismissed." He simply knew Carter wouldn't come back unless it was "the very best job he could do." He was not satisfied with as-good-as or so-so's.

So it is with top salespeople. They are like an artist finishing a painting and then deciding there is a little more blue needed in the sky. The writer editing his script for the fifth time and finally finding a sought -after word that changes the mood and meaning. The businessman who says, "When I walk in my store/office I can feel rhythm. When the rhythm is smooth and easy, I know things are working well. When the rhythm is jagged and uneven I know there's a problem to solve."

Good salespeople seek to surpass what they have done before. They repeat what worked, but demand a higher goal. They read, they watch, they observe, they listen. They know there are even taller peaks to climb that can be conquered only by working towards. . . perfection.

Summary

1. *Hard working*
2. *Self confident*
3. *Self disciplined*
4. *Perseverance*
5. *Flexibility*
6. *Goals other than money*
7. *Respect for the buyer's good sense*
8. *Willingness to learn from others*
9. *Ability to handle big money*
10. *Perfectionist*

28 First Class Is The Only Way To Go

It all began in a hotel room in New York City four years ago. The overnight rate was a "special for buyers." But the room was tiny, cramped, and overlooked a ventilation shaft. They had mirrored one wall to make the room look larger.

"We want a bigger room," we said, "with a view of the park."

"That will cost more," said the bellhop, "This is the room for the special rate."

We felt the "special" rate was not special. We moved. Our new room was larger and we awoke in the morning with a park panorama outside our window. Our starting-the-day attitude was high. We felt good. First class.

Later, we thought about what had happened. We suddenly realized we had traveled through much of our lives as "second-class" citizens. Searching for the lowest price instead of the highest quality.

Perhaps this was a throwback to our childhood scrunching up small in the railroad seat to pass as "under 12" and a cheaper fare.

Perhaps it was going out to dinner and knowing we were expected to order the least expensive entree.

This conditioning as children influenced our thinking as adults. And then we asked ourselves: Why be second rate in our buying and in our advertising?

Why not "travel" first class?

But, we do not associate the words "first class" with "making money." One follows the other in that order.

Philip Wrigley once said, "My father was never particularly interested in making money. He always said if you do the right thing and build your bridges strong, making money will come automatically."

What we are talking about is 1) attitude, and 2) mind-set.

Attitude: Offering first-class service means attracting more business. Don't your customers react positively if they are treated first-class? (Answer: Yes!)

How they are treated determines not only if they will return but when. How often. And most important how much they will spend.

The Japanese call a customer "o-kyaku-san." It means "visitor to one's home." They believe all work is sacred. And so the bellhop, the waiter, the housekeeper all take pride in doing not only a good job but a job . . . "First-class."

It make sense says Yoshihisa Senoh, chief of employee training at Tokyo's 152-year-old Takashimaya department store, "When you have guests to your home, you clean the entrance and prepare the rooms. We invite 'guests' every day to our store. We have to make them comfortable when they shop."

And they do. From the time you enter the store and young women greet you with a bow and softly say "irrashaimase" (translation: "welcome") until the moment you leave with each purchase painstakingly and attractively gift-wrapped with the store's logo and signature colors. First-class.

Mind-set: Joe Girard, America's number one automobile salesman wears a gold pin in the shape of the number one on his lapel. He bought it at the local jewelry store. When people see the pin they day, "What's that for?"

He says, "It's because I'm number one."

His theory: How can a customer have confidence in him unless he has confidence in himself? Being number one creates an awareness, a certain mystique which travels as a companion to confidence. And confidence comes from a continuing mind-set to be. . . first class.

First class does not only mean the upfront seat in the airplane or the top deck in the ocean liner. That is only the end result which will happen once you begin to think/act/decide what you do in your work, your life, in your day-to-day activity will be . . . first-class.

No one really wants to be a second-class person.

No one really wants to do a second-class job.

Why aspire to be the salutatorian of the class when the valedictorian job is open?

People work, function, perform, first-class because of how they believe. No matter where they are. Martin Luther King writes a powerful statement and creates a movement from a Birmingham jail, and Anne Frank leaves an indelible memory from a diary written in hiding on the top floor of her Amsterdam home.

Do you continually aspire, yearn, strive?

Yes, your store/office is well-kept and the flower boxes planted and the street washed down. Your mailing pieces are known to be attractive and immediately identifiable. But soon all this becomes a "given." And we are content with what-we-are and not with what-we-might-be. Humorist Josh Billings once wrote, "One of the rarer things a man ever does is to do the best he can."

Simply having a reputation for quality is not enough to sustain your business, much less have it grow. You must, as the original slogan for N.W. Ayer advertising said, "Keep everlastingly at it." To do as your predecessors did and no more is to wind up with a marvelous reputation. . . and no customers. And Best and Company and Abercrombie and Fitch go out of business.

It is a little bit like the punch line in the burlesque routine, "But what have you done for me lately?"

Having a background, tradition and reputation is fine, commendable and to-be-wished. But today's generation did not know your father or grandfather. As the Irish say, "You've got to do your own growing—no matter how tall your grandfather was."

And so the question is, "Do you want to go first-class?" (Can we have a show of hands?) Good. Starting today, make that your goal: to achieve first-class—in personal achievement, in attitude toward customers, in your mailing piece that conveys who-you-are to your customer.

Remember it was Orphan Annie who said, "Ya hafta earn what you get. . . "

29

The Five Magic Words of Selling

It was Gawaine le Coeur-Hardy who gave me the idea.

I met him in the classic short story by Heywood Brown, "The Fifty-First Dragon."

Gawaine was a promising student in the school of dragon-slaying. On the eve of his graduation he was assigned to kill a dragon eating the lettuce in the school's garden.

Gawaine demurred, said he wasn't ready and asked for an "enchanted cap" to make himself invisible when the dragon appeared.

The headmaster reassured him offering something far better than the magic cap— a magic word! All Gawaine had to do was say the magic word and he could cut off the dragon's head at leisure.

The magic word: "Rumplesnitz."

Gawaine memorized the word and killed 50 dragons. On his next trip to the forest he forgot the word and was never heard from again.

Is there such a word or combination of words that would also work in selling?

Is there some magic phase that, once applied, would result in increased sales, higher profits, bigger cars and longer vacations?

Is there some combination of vowels and consonants that once learned, could be taught to others and increase the sales of goods and services and contribute to the economic well being of the country in which we live?

Yes.

They were not easy to find. We researched the successful advertisements. We looked over direct mail pieces that pulled out of proportion. We listened very carefully to words of the best salespeople as they totalled record breaking sales. We read the books of the experts.

And we found the common denominator.

Every successful person-to-person sale, every good-pulling ad, every record-breaking direct mailer had a distinct, obvious and specific appeal from the seller to buyer. We found pocketbooks were opened faster, credit cards handed over more quickly and above all, an enthusiasm for buying on the part of the customer if one simple phrase were answered properly.

These are the magic five words. **"What's in it for me?"**

Now the customer knows what's in it for **you** when they purchase your product or service. You take their money and put it in your register.

But what's in it for them?

Why should they buy your merchandise, spend for your services, take home your advertised item?

Why should they walk past the thousands of advertised brands in the supermarket and choose your brand for their shopping basket? What makes their weary eyes, seeing hundreds of commercials daily on newspapers, TV, billboards and magazines, suddenly snap alert when your name appears?

The magic five words: "What's in it for me?"

• Does the headline in your ad promise a benefit?

• Does the sub headline repeat that benefit and explain it more fully or add another reason-to-buy?

• Does the final closing paragraph inform the reader/viewer what will happen if they do not act immediately? To take advantage of an offer they can't refuse?

Direct mail has a head start with these five magic words over all other advertising media. It has a built-in advantage: a me and thee relationship between buyer and seller not present, available or functional in any other medium.

Direct mail goes directly to the customer. It establishes a close relationship and says or implies this offer is something special. Between you and me. Not available to the rest of the world.

Your customer knows your mailing piece offers them something alone, different, unique. They know the mailing piece is not available to the newspaper or radio or TV to be viewed and read by the vast audience of everyone. The mailing piece is for someone. By its very nature, it answers the question: "What's in it for me?"

They feel a mailing piece is personal, a relationship unattainable by another media.

And it's true.

Imagine going on a date for the first time with a very nice woman in your community. It would be most natural for you to write her the following day and say, "I enjoyed being with you last night. I hope we shall be together again in the future." The girl would smile when reading, tuck it in her pocketbook and think how nice it was for you to send the note.

Now, imagine instead of writing a note, you take out a newspaper ad with the same message. Or have the local radio announcer broadcast the same phrases as a commercial.

The girl would be astonished, angry, embarrassed, bewildered, lock herself in her room with an imagined attack of the flu and most certainly would never never speak to you again. What happened?

The same message was delivered to her all three times.

One time she was flattered. The other two times outraged.

Why? Because the direct mail piece was to her alone. It was personal. It answered the what's-in-it-for-me question on a one-to-one basis. And it worked. The other ways did not.

What this proves: The more you take care of your customer on a one-to-one basis, the more successful your business.

Bob Davis of Davis Supermarkets outside Pittsburgh, spends the first hour his store is opened at the front door greeting his customers. He knows many by name and asks about their children, their family and certain food products he remembered they recently purchased.

The surrounding chain stores are no threat to Bob Davis. He has successfully answered the question, "What's in it for me?"

In a small market in Madisonville, Kentucky, the Edwards brothers, Tom and Hayden, outdistance their 18 competitors in retail food sales. They simply show their customers they care.

At the busiest hours of the day, one of the brothers is at the check-out counter asking each customer, "Did you find everything you wanted today?" If the answer is "No" and it's for something in stock, a runner is nearby to fetch the wanted item. If it's not in stock they take the name and phone number and call when it arrives.

The competition can't touch them. They care. They answer the "What's in it for me" question every time customers shop their store.

Once you learn these magic words, do not simply pay their lip service. You must act them out on an every day basis so the words turn into habits.

Otherwise you will find yourself with the problem of Gawaine le Coeur-Hardy. When he knew what to do he succeeded. But when he forgot . . . he failed.

30 *How Listening Can Increase Your Sales*

The salesman called on the drug store every week to fill inventories and check new items. He always greeted the owner with a big smile and the question, "Good to see you. How's the family?"

The store owner answered "Fine," and the salesman replied, "Terrific. Let me show you what we have for you this week."

Wondering if the salesman really cared about his family, the owner decided to give him a new answer. The salesman showed up on schedule the following week and said, "Glad to see you. How's the family?"

The owner said, "Well, my mother-in-law jumped off the cliff, the children are lost in a forest and my wife had to go to a leper colony."

Without missing a beat the salesman answered, "Terrific. Let me show you what we have for you this week."

What happened?

The salesman was so concerned about making the sale he wasn't listening to his customer. He forgot the basic rule in selling: **Find out what the customer wants and give it to them.**

But you can't find out if you don't listen.

Major corporations are learning this fast. Look through national magazines. You will find large double-truck ads from these firms saying they take the time to listen to their customers.

"Before we designed the BMC computers, we listened."

— BMC Division of Technology Group

"We hear you. We're doing a lot of listening these days at P & G."

— Procter and Gamble.

"When you told us nobody could understand your business like people in your business. . . we listened."

— Unisys

All of us in selling are usually so concerned with getting across our selling message ("Terrific. Let me show you what we have for you this week") we don't take the time to listen to what the customer wants.

This means listening **to**. Not **against**.

When you listen **against** you are not listening. You are simply, politely, patiently waiting for the customer to finish what he or she is saying so you can leap into what you want to say, which, too often has no relationship to what the customer just said. ("My children are lost in a forest.")

Unless you take the time to listen, you cannot communicate. Listening is the most used communication skill, but the least taught.

A hostess once invited a certain man to all her parties. Everyone said they enjoyed him so much. But the hostess was mystified. The man was no life of the party. He was, in fact quiet and subdued. What quality did he have she missed?

At the next party she introduced him to one of her guests and then hovered nearby to over hear his technique. It was very simple. After being introduced he would ask his new acquaintance, "Tell me about yourself. . . " and then just listen.

He listened to everyone talk about themselves. He encouraged them to tell him about their jobs, their family, their hopes, their dreams. Where would they like to go on their next vacation, and why? And for how long?

Later everyone told the hostess what a marvelous addition he was to the party.

Why? Because people who listen seem to care more, seem more open-minded and concerned. Those who continually talk come across as pompous, self-centered and often narrow-minded. They interrupt, they criticize (without having fully listened to the complete story), they earn a bad — and often undeserved — reputation.

Unisys (remember their headline a few paragraphs back?) runs listening seminars. They actually teach their salespeople and management how-to-listen.

"Listening" they say, "is more than hearing. It's our primary method of receiving information."

They point out people hear words but you have to listen for the meaning of the words.

If you "listen well" you not only hear the sounds of words but you also see the physical movement of people when they talk. You hear the tone of their voice. You see their body movement. The way they wear their clothes.

OK, what does listening have to do with your business?

A lot. Because we are all in the business of communication. If we have a telephone marketing setup and are not listening to nuances, phrases, exact information, we wind up apologizing, rewriting orders, apologizing, reshipping merchandise, apologizing, remaking appointments, apologizing. . .

How can we make sure what we say is accurately read, heard and acted upon?

Here are a few guidelines:

1. Is what you're saying what the customer wants to hear?

A midwestern bank put together a rough of a customer mailing inviting them to the bank's million dollar remodeling party. The brochure spoke of the marble floor from Italy, the ultrasonic elevators, the new computers, the expensive carpeting. Then someone on the staff asked, "How is the customer helped by our spending their money?"

His point: Take all the features and translate them into customer benefits. No long teller lines. Answers on loans in one day. Quick 24-hour banking. Less ego talk, more customer talk. Then they will listen. Come. Buy.

2. Are you listening to what your customer is saying?

Isn't that what testing is all about? If you send 1,000 mailers for

a new product to your customer list and only 1 percent buy —
you change the product. Or the offer. Or the creative. Or the
timing. Something! Otherwise you are not listening.

3. Practice listening.

Listening is conditioning and habit-forming. Start today by
forcing yourself to completely listen — really listen to whatever
anyone is talking to you about. Look them in the eyes. Hear them
out. Do not let your mind wonder which is easy since we hear
four times faster than people speak. Concentrate. You are teaching
yourself how to respond quickly, automatically and efficiently in
face-to-face and letter-to-letter selling.

4. Accept new ideas.

Just because a selling pattern or written copy worked before
does **not** mean it cannot be improved. Watch what is happening
in the news to sense a shift in national trends, mores, style. A Wall
Street commodities firm has outstanding success because they
decided not to specialize in one commodity as do most experts.

They spent two years assembling data that convinced them
commodity prices around the world are interrelated. That
weather conditions around the world are interrelated. That
weather conditions on the Falkland Islands can affect the price of
wool which can affect the price of gold in Tokyo. They feel they
must **listen** to everything, everyday to continue their record of
success.

5. Be patient.

Listen all-the-way-through. Otherwise you react too quickly.
You anticipate. You change directions so quickly you can lose
your firm's identification in the marketplace.

So, listen very carefully. Starting today. It will result in larger
sales, bigger profits, or, at the very least, receiving invitations to
all the best parties in town.

31

Here's the Basic Rule in Selling: Give Your Customers What they Want.

In the Seaman's Bethel Church in New Bedford, Massachusetts, the pulpit is shaped like a ship's bow. Just as it's described in the novel **Moby Dick.**

But it wasn't always so.

Visitors to New Bedford used to walk through the church asking whatever happened to the ship's bow pulpit described in the novel.

The truth is, there never was one. Herman Melville just added the touch as artistic license.

But so many people came and asked, the church rebuilt its pulpit. . . into the shape of a ship's bow!

This illustrates a basic rule in selling: Find out what the customer wants. . . and give it to them. (which we have emphasized several times in this book because of its importance.)

How does this rule work in **your** business?

We all have known retailers who begin in business saying, "I'm going to buy what I like for my store. If the customers don't like it, well, too bad."

Well, too bad for the retailer. He soon folds up his tent and is vaguely remembered as one of the approximately 35,000 who go out of business every year.

We have come a long way in merchandising since Henry Ford was asked what color he planned to offer his model T's. "Give them any color they want," said Henry "as long as it's black."

Today the stores or showrooms are chock-full of a wide variety of color and style and selection from which your customer can pick and choose.

The problem is — and always has been — how do we **really** know what our customer wants?

A mini skirt selection today could be a maxi mistake.

Yesterday's Ray Eberle is today's Bruce Springsteen.

And somewhere in this promised land there are warehouses full of men's Nehru shirts and women's satin hot pants waiting for the style to return. Someday. Maybe. Great ideas whose time has come. . . and gone.

People's taste and style and choice of what they want to eat, wear, read or participate in continually changes. Some gradually. Some overnight. But we can be sure the only thing that remains constant. . . is change.

How can you, as a business person, plan to buy not just what-you-like but, more important, what your customer likes?

One way: Test.

Seat of the pants merchandising and eye-balling the store to see what is selling is no longer enough in our increasing competitive and high interest money economy.

When a piece of merchandise sells well, the buyer is quick to be recognized as the one who made the decision and quick to claim the credit.

When a piece of merchandise does **not** sell well it is the fault of the manufacturer ("He changed it from when I bought it"), the salesman ("He is high pressure, you know"), or the timing ("We're just ahead of everybody else"). 'Tis true indeed that victory has many parents, and defeat is an orphan.

We can narrow the defeats, increase the wins and be thought of as the person to hire, the store to shop or the business to patronize if we simply "test" what we offer the public before we make major commitments.

Department stores do this all the time. They strike fear in the heart of suppliers with, "We'll try a few dozen. If it clicks, we expect you to fill orders at once."

Great for department stores. Disaster for the small specialty shop who does not have the clout or impact to back up these demands.

How do you "test" in your store? Here's a 1-2-3 guide:

1. Advertise an item in small space far enough in advance of its peak season to see customer reaction.

2. Do a whole series of these small ads. Keep careful tabulation of how many sold. In what color. What sizes, etc.

3. Run these ads in the same section of the paper so they are an effective "control" on one another. Placing one ad in the sport section and another in the society page attracts different readers. You lose track of who's buying what.

What have you done?

You are simply finding out what your customer wants to buy. A true story of how this works: One Christmas we ran a series of small newspaper ads on gift clothing for all members of the family from infants through grandparents.

We thought each item was a winner since we had bought them. But what would the customer choose as winners?

Some of the ads were an immediate success. Some were not.

A week before Christmas we took the 14 best selling, and now **tested** items, and repeated them in a full page ad with the headline: "Here's 14 last-minute ideas for holiday gifts. . ." We listed a telephone number for direct response.

Cost of the ad: $1,200.

The phone began ringing as soon as the store opened. By one o'clock, there was more than $3,000 in orders — enough profit to pay for the ad. Within two days, orders for the 14 items totalled nearly $10,000.

Most amazing fact: Each item pulled more orders when run this second time in the full-page ad than they did when originally run by themselves. (Winners begat winners).

Which merely proves success in marketing is simply finding out what your customers wants. . . and giving it to them.

32 The Psychology of The Second Interest

Crackerjack sales are at an all-time high.

But one of their big problems is finding new, different and inexpensive toys to tuck inside the box with the caramel popcorn. The makers of Crackerjack know one of the reasons sales are high is because many of the customers want the prize. . . . not the product.

The Arthritis Foundation in Southern New Jersey wanted to raise a lot of money. But how many people would come to another charity luncheon? They invited baseball superstar, Philadelphia's Tug McGraw, to speak. Result: $25,000 raised for the charity. The tickets ranged up to $50 apiece and sold because of the celebrity. . . not the cause.

Famed designer Ralph Lauren, makes a lightweight woman's zip front casual jacket that sells for about $60. But if you buy his Lauren fragrance you can have a comparable windbreaker for $20. Customers flocked to buy, figuring the sale made sense as well as scents.

This technique of selling— offering another product to have you buy the main product is a theory we call, "The Psychology of the Second Interest" (PSI).

What that means: You can often have the customer buy the product you want them to buy by creating an interest in another product they want to buy. The second interest. . . sells the first.

You see it work in direct mail pieces received daily.

Publisher's Clearinghouse offers houses and a lifetime income in their annual subscription appeal. (And, by the way folks, we're also selling magazines.)

Now, you may not be a magazine reader. In fact, you don't even have to buy the magazines to be eligible for the contest. But possessing the basic America savvy of you don't get nothin' for nothin', you figure the odds of winning are greatly increased if you just happen to buy a few magazines. Why not? When the prize is a house. Or a lifetime income. You can **always** read the magazines, somewhere, sometime. . .

What have you done? Succumbed to PSI. The "second interest," the money or the house, caused you to buy the magazine first.

Is your business having a convention? Well, it certainly is educational for you to go and learn what's new and different in your profession. The mailing piece lists the activities and seminars. Just sign up to attend. Whatever doubts you have disappear when you see the convention is in Las Vegas. Or New Orleans. Or Atlanta. Or Boca Raton. Or San Francisco.

Honestly now, would you sign up as quickly if the meeting was held in Dubuque?*

The PSI of Fun City made you buy the original offer.

Take a moment and go through the boxes of cereal and groceries on your kitchen shelves. Post Grape Nuts offers you the chance to **Team up with Bob Griese (former Miami Dolphins Quarterback) and win free athletic equipment for your school.**

All you do is save the "Fun 'n Fitness seals" on the side of the cereal box or from any of your other Post favorites: Log Cabin syrup, Orange Plus drinks and Wonder bread. Now, if you can convince the entire school population to munch Grape Nuts and drink Orange Plus for breakfast every morning, you could outfit the gymnasium in a few months.

* Old speaker's joke: "Dubuque? It's not the end of the world. But you can see it from there."

Pick a pack of Del Monte raisins, tear off the top label and you can have a $15 embossed hard cover Rand McNally World Atlas (over 300 pages with more than 190 in full color)— **for half price**.

A carton of Land O' Lakes butter is valuable not just for what's inside but also what's outside. There, on the package, in an "exclusive offer" for a new Chicken & Seafood cookbook for $1.25 and proof-of-purchase.

The average supermarket carries 29,000 different items. Hundreds do not sell their features or benefits. Instead, they advertise what you can **also** get **if** you buy the product. . .

A lack of enlistment in the nation's military forces promoted the hiring of advertising agencies. They immediately launched into the PSI technique by asking if you would like a free college education or travel at no expense. You would? All you have to do is sign your name on the bottom of this three-year commitment.

A variation of this technique is to offer an item **related** to the object to be sold, but not necessarily in the same family. Like all relatives, some are interesting to have and others you simply ignore.

The owner of a condominium does not show you four walls, a ceiling and a floor. He hires a designer, who fills the room with attractive furniture. When you examine the room-for-sale you are impressed with the total "look" and you buy. Only when you walk into what you bought and see the emptiness do you realize what made you buy was not the four walls, ceiling and floor. . . but the furniture.

The shoe salesman convinces you the $ 1 polish will make your shoes last longer, remain soft, supple and constantly look new. This $ 1 polish "related" sale often sells the $50 shoes.

The clothing salesman sees you hesitating to spend $300 for the suit. He quickly matches up the appropriate shirt and tie to show the "complete package." You are impressed with the shirt and tie and wind up buying the suit (and then, of course, the shirt and tie that made you buy the suit for the ultimate wrap-around sale).

And so, students, when putting together your next mailing, consider the Psychology of the Second Interest. After you have carefully written an opening headline to have them open the envelope, listed all the advantages why they should buy now, close with an effective P.S. with extra savings by ordering in the next 10 days and reminding them one more time with an "In case you have decided **not** to order . . . " Publisher's letter, try one more technique: Offer something other than and not related to that which you are trying to sell.

And the next time you come to visit, I'll show you my all-brass bookmark from Literary Guild. Has my initials on it. I show it to everyone. Very attractive. Oh, yes, the books I had to buy **are** in the house too.

Somewhere.

33
Every Crisis is an Opportunity in Disguise

The Chinese word for "crisis" has two characters. One means "Danger." But the other one means "Opportunity."

In these difficult economic times, many businesses find themselves in the classic position of one-step-forwards, two-steps-backwards. They fight for an annual increase to at least equal the jumping cost of living. Business often becomes a case of treading water which means running in place. . . and going nowhere.

Some retailers, faced with less customers or the same customer spending less, wring their hands and, like Chicken Little, look heavenward expecting the sky to come tumbling down.

Other retailers break apart the "crisis" to seek out the "opportunity."

Retailers in business for the past quarter century remember the good old days when being a merchant simply meant opening the shop, marking the goods and collecting the dollars. Competition, especially in price, was non-existent. They were protected by Fair Trade laws. If they sold a General Electric clock at $9.95, everyone sold the same clock at the same price.

Suddenly, in the 1960's there was a "Retailing Revolution." Entrepreneurs moved into New England mills abandoned by manufacturers for the lower wages of the South.

Suddenly, these empty buildings became "Discount Mills," chock-full of merchandise available at your friendly neighborhood store — but at lower prices.

The retailer counter-attacked. "Foul," they cried and took these new competitors to court. "Fair Trade laws," they yelled and asked the judges to make those terrible people stop selling their merchandise at those terrible low prices.

Surprise. The Supreme Court ruled Fair Trade was not fair. And whatever happened to the good old American tradition of free enterprise anyhow?

Retailers were shocked.

Some responded by saying, "Anything you can sell, I can sell cheaper. I can sell anything cheaper than you. . ."

Not true.

The discounter came back cheaper than cheap. And the small retailer, unable to compete, folded his retailing tent and wondered whatever happened to the good old American dream of being your own boss.

It was still there. But the dream turned into a nightmare, and many retailers never woke up.

Some did.

They went to New York City and saw something most amazing. Lord and Taylor and Saks Fifth Avenue and Bergdorf Goodman and Bloomingdales were still in business. They did not have large paper signs taped on their big windows saying they were the cheapest in town. They did not use price as their primary selling point. They did not have large sale racks and tables all over their first floors.

Just the opposite.

They decided they had a particular niche to fill. That all customers were not alike. That many did **not** choose price as the **first** consideration.

There existed an audience that sought selection and service and signs of excitement that good retailing, like theatre, conveys. And they succeeded.

Wow! Could the small retailer do that?

Sure. The first thing they had to figure out was **how** to do that.

Soon the retailer realized the whole world was not his customer. That to be successful, his business future must be tied to projecting a particular image to a particular group. Not the entire universe of shoppers. But to one potential universe.

Enter direct marketing.

The retailer quickly learned it is far, far easier to attract more dollars from the customer he has than to attract a new customer. Easier. And less expensive.

The retailer quickly learned he could not become all things to all people but rather a specific thing to as specific person.

And the retailer quickly learned he could best do all this by. . . direct marketing.

Those that learned, succeeded and prospered. Yes, business was more difficult. Yes, buying was more intense. Yes, attention had to be paid on a more personal level. But they were survivors.

Now, let us consider the banking industry.

Twenty years after the retailer learned this lesson in economics, the banks and savings and loans were still carrying on the marketing traditions of yesterday. The basic 4 percent passbook interest rate was still paid by banks (with one-quarter percent more by the S & Ls). The 20 and 30 year, 5 percent home mortgages were cast in concrete and would exist forever. Competition was so keen some banks offered automobile loans as low as 3 percent to hold and attract customers.

Suddenly, the federal government with its ever-expanding consumer-oriented deregulation policy hit the financial market.

Suddenly, there was open warfare on interest rates.

Suddenly, the fair and equitable longstanding interest rates that rarely varied one quarter of one percent over the course of a year. . . changed. Fair and equitable meant the rules changed. Fair and equitable meant every man (or bank) for himself. Fair and equitable meant what was fair and equitable for the customer. . . **not** the banker. (What happened to the good old days? Look, the sky is really falling **now**!)

It was a crisis situation.

Some financial institutions, still wanting to do business with everyone, saw their reserves dwindle. Others were gobbled up by the bigger fish in the sea.

But the survivors, the ones who saw the opportunities, said, "Wait. I can handle this. I will go after the particular market where I am best suited."

And so a small bank in Rome, Georgia, concentrated on senior citizens. They offer free bus rides for sightseeing, entertainment in their senior citizen complexes, transportation to supermarkets. They are identified as the "senior citizens" bank for all those nice folk with big balances that want to keep their money where someone cares about them.

American automobile sales are at a low level. Auto dealers go out of business weekly. The industry wisely decided to spend even more on advertising because business is bad. But, the most remarkable statement was by Donald Peterson, president of Ford Motor company on the front page of Advertising Age, the bible of the ad industry. He said, "The time is past when one can create a single mass message and reach millions of consumers effectively. We must look increasingly for matching media that will enable us best to reach carefully targeted emerging markets of the 1980's. The rifle approach rather than the old shotgun."

It seems as though Confucious was right. For if one of the Chinese symbols for Crisis is opportunity, is the other. . . direct mail?

34 The Rule of Three: To Grab Attention, Hold Interest And Influence Buying

Is there a simple rule to writing successful copy?

Here's one:

Say what you're going to say.

Say it.

Say what you said.

It works.

Look closely at the formula. It has three parts. Each one leads you into the next and when you finish you have a complete story.

We call this: The Rule of Three.

The dictionary says this rule has a mathematical background and means "The method of finding the fourth term in a proportion when three terms are given."

Really? What 's **that** mean?

This: When you put together three parts of a problem, the fourth becomes obvious.

We find the Rule of Three works for us to grab attention, hold interest and influence buying.

We once wrote of the "rhythm of writing." Good prose is really good free verse. You can read it from a stage with a beat and movement and direction that has a strong influence of the subconscious.

If you mention one fact, it stands alone. Mention two and they are awkward, like waiting for another shoe to drop. But write in terms of three examples, testimonials, real-life happenings, and the reader "believes" more strongly than otherwise.

Why is that?

No specific reason. It's like tearing apart the rattle to see what makes the noise. If you examine it too closely you might destroy the reason-why.

Perhaps it's because we use expressions of three in our every day life. The rhythm and sound and balance make the same application in what you write more believable, because the reader has been down that road before and recognizes the path and is comfortable going along with you.

Think of children's rhymes and you will remember the number of Old King Cole's fiddlers, the three men in the tub and how much wool the black sheep had.

A young lady uses the rule in terms of potential dates (Tom, Dick & Harry), what she hopes they will look like (tall, dark and handsome) and the name of the auto supply business where they work (Manny, Moe and Jack).

A young man soon discovers three is a crowd when he's only interested in wine, and women and song. If he then selects one lady, he wants a loaf of bread, a jug of wine and thou.

We start school saluting our flag with its red, white and blue and learn to color with the three primary colors. Then we start with reading, 'riting and 'rithmetic and graduate into reading Caesar's Roman history with its memorable first sentence that all Gaul is divided into three parts. We learn a little history about Columbus arriving with the Nina, Pinta and Santa Maria. We take time out to watch TV, see the Three Stooges and Donald's rambunctious nephews, Huey, Dewey and Louie. Or switch to the baseball where you're out with three strikes. (Because of a triple play?)

A course on religion takes you from Three Wise Men to the Holy Trinity and informs us about the excommunication ceremony that began in the Eighth century with bell, book and candle.

Study three-act plays of the theatre with each story having a beginning, middle and end. Directors practice the rule of stage triangulation so each actor can not only be seen but also convey emotions by the different strains put on the triangular movement.

In higher education, we examine the philosophy of George Hegel and his theory of Thesis, Antithesis and Synthesis (Translation: State the problem, consider its opposite meaning, then blend the two into a final solution). And, of course, Freudian psychology with his "three tyrants:" Id, Ego and Super Ego.

Throughout life everyone we meet seems to fall into one of three categories, according to Harvard Professor David McClellan. He says people can be categorized into *Achievers, Affiliators and Power People*.

How that helps you: If you can pinpoint your audience, it makes the selling of your product much easier. Soon you know which category your customer fits and you sell appropriately.

Here's how to recognize three categories:

Achievers are self-starters. Goal setters. They know what they want to do. They make decisions and "work the options" all the time.

Never tell an achiever, "There is only one way to do this."

"Really?" they'll say. . . and then give you three more! (Yes, three. . .) They are great for working lunch, working breakfasts and working late.

They are not subtle. If you are not making the grade, they tell you. They are always measuring, taking stock, examining carefully. Themselves and those around them. They hate surprises. "No surprises," they say and then, "no disappointments."

Affiliators are the corporate men. IBM, MGM, RCA, AT&T, NBC, CBS, ABC, (and did you notice they all have three initials? You did? Good, you're catching on. . .) They are important cogs in the business world and keep things moving.

They are patient. And builders. And belongers. The service clubs and bowling teams. Good people to have on your team because they tend the store and watch the register while you are away planning a particular promotion.

Power People say "This is my desk," and "Did you notice the trophies on the wall," or "See the famous people with me in these pictures!" Yes, they are good managers, competent executives and important leaders, but they like special perks, like club membership, first-class travel and company travel card.

They are organized, on time and make decisions quickly (which is how they got the biggest desks in the largest rooms in the corner location). They have the title. . . and the respect.

Approach them with facts and figures at the ready. Unlike affiliators, they make decisions quickly but want the backup data and statistics. Make your first pitch a good one. You may not have a second chance.

So when preparing your next marketing piece, remember the Rule of Three when writing your copy. List three benefits, three reasons-to-buy and three ways to purchase and your sales will increase. Well, at least threefold. Which, at this stage of your reading should certainly be as easy as, uh. . . 1-2-3 .

35

Can You Guess The Name of The Mystery Guest?

"We're going to play a real fun game tonight," said the hostess as the guests arrived.

After dinner she explained the game.

Each person would have someone's name taped to his/her back. He or she would ask anyone in the room questions about this person. Each had ten minutes to try to guess the name of the "mystery" person.

The famous ones were easy. The movie stars took only a few minutes. But half way through the evening, one person simply could not guess the name on his back. He asked all the right questions, and, finally, at the ten-minute mark, gave up.

"Don't you have any idea who the person could be?" asked the hostess.

"No" he replied. "None of the descriptions or answers seemed in the least bit familiar."

The hostess took off the name and showed it to him.

It was his own.

What happened?

This: Each of us have an image of who we are to ourselves that does not necessarily correspond to who we are to others.

This **point of view concept** is important to remember in marketing. For if we are marketing directly to an individual (and we are) we must understand **his or her** point of view before we write our copy.

Example: A bank in northern California wanted to increase its advertising budget.

"First thing," said the advertising agency the bank hired, "we want to know your present customer. That is your basic strength. You'll grow from there."

Management agreed. The advertising team first interviewed the Chief Executive Officer. "Tell us," they said to him, "who is your typical customer."

The chairman quickly answered, "That's easy. Most are in their 60's headed for retirement and make a comfortable income."

Really?

Next they went to middle management asking the same question. The reply: "They're in their 40's, have a couple of kids in college or about to go there, and just starting to make a good income."

Really?

Their next stop — the tellers.

"Sure. They're in their late teens or early twenties. Just starting out. Hoping to make a career in their new jobs."

What happened?

Each person related the "average" customer to himself. From his point of view, the customer was — himself. That was his point of view.

When putting together your next direct marketing idea, think in terms of your audience and the benefits **they** want. Not you.

In Al Reis' classic book on Positioning, he gives the Cadillac automobile as an example of how this works. From the customer's point of view, the Cadillac is a big comfortable car. From General Motors' point of view, the Cadillac is their most profitable vehicle.

Which point of view do you think they stress in their marketing?

You were born in the North. You know what happened during the Civil War. You learned later in life the victors write history books, but there was no denying the greatness of Lincoln, his fight to save the Union and to free the slaves from the South. You were conditioned and your point of view established.

But take a walk up Commerce Street in Austin, Texas. You will see a statue of Jefferson Davis in front of the state capital. There, inscribed on the base of the statue, are these words:

DIED

For state's rights guaranteed under the Constitution. The people of the South, animated by the Spirit of '76 to preserve their rights, withdrew from the Federal compact in 1861. The North resorted to coercion. The South, against overwhelming numbers and resources, fought until exhausted. Number of men enlisted: Confederate, 437,000. Federal 485,216.

Really? Up to that moment your point of view was the South were the bad guys. But their point of view was they died for "state's rights" and withdrew from the Union because of the "Spirit of '76" and "to preserve their right." Pretty convincing. . .

Listen to an artist and copywriter working on a direct mailing piece. Or an ad.

The artist: "There's too much copy. You're not leaving any room for my art."

The writer: "Cut the picture down. Without the copy no one will know what we're selling. I have to get all the basic information in the ad."

The artist says the picture sells the product. The writer says the words sell the product. **Point of view.**

Some tire salesmen feel they should tell customers about how the steel belted tires are made and the seven cords of steel wrapped together to form strong reinforcement.

The woman driver wants to hear about the tire being safe when she takes her children to school.

The salesman is talking about construction, when he should be talking about safety.

The travel agent doesn't sell the time payment to pay off the airline tickets. They sell the romance, the glamour, the excitement.

The clothing salesman doesn't sell the stitches to the inch. He sells fashion, style, the appeal to the opposite sex.

Point of view.

We once made a speech in Toronto. The audience was in the business of selling food.

We asked the sponsor if the audience was composed of retailers. He assured us it was.

We did a program that worked for us successfully many times in the past. This time it did not. Several people actually walked out. The applause was polite but unenthusiastic.

A friend came out of the audience to say how much he enjoyed the show.

"Are you sure?" we asked. "The audience did not seem to share your enthusiasm."

"I noticed that," he answered, "and I can't figure out why you gave that speech on retailers who own their own food store. You see, the audience was all **wholesalers.**"

Wrong point of view. I was on stage telling them how to greet customers, how to run promotions, how to do direct marketing all from a retail point of view. They could care less. They were wholesalers. Not retailers.

What say the wise men of direct marketing?

First comes the list and the offer. All else follows.

Once we have the list and the offer, the marketing piece must address itself to that audience. Their fears, their hopes, their wishes, their most wanted desires. Only when we approach what we sell from the customer's point of view will we be successful.

The best salespeople approach a client in their office by first carefully looking around the room. The pictures or trophies on the wall. The collectables on the desk. They start the conversation about one of these items — the customer's interest not their own.

When you approach a sale from the customer's point of view instead of your own, you are in the position of the young boy, looking through a telescope for the first time who can't believe how small everything looks.

Then he is told to turn the telescope around. Now he has a broader picture.

He has, in fact, a more comprehensive. . . **point of view.**

36

Don't Answer Customers' Questions With More Questions.

We went into the New York showroom to buy a new line. The salesman approached us. We said, "Hi. This is the first time we're buying this line. So we'd like some advice on colors, style, and fashion direction. Can you help us?"

He answered, "You know there's a minimum of 200 pieces you have to buy before we'll sell you . . . "

Was that the answer to our question?

We easily could buy two or three times his minimum. . .

IF the merchandise was what we wanted. . .

IF he was willing to help us pick and choose. . .

IF he answered our question with, "Sure. Terrific. We're excited you store is interested in us. . ."

And then somewhere, someplace, sometime as the sale progresses and the order blank fills, **then** ask us if their minimum quantity fill **our** needs (not theirs).

His approach was one of how not to sell rather than how to sell us . . . more!

Taking care of the customer you have is your guarantee for increased sales.

And speaking of guarantees. . .

What happens when your customer returns merchandise to your store, and your philosophy, policy and procedure is you

guarantee what you sell? This should mean when something is returned, you replace the merchandise or refund the money. No questions asked.

What actually happens, is, sadly, exactly the opposite.

Most retailers ask questions instead of simply giving a simple answer.

If the customer says, "I'm unhappy with this merchandise because. . ."

1. "The colors ran in the wash."
2. "It doesn't fit properly."
3. "The color looks bad on me."
4. None of the above.

Most retailers respond with an inquisitive inquisition:

1. "Did you wash it in cold water?"
2. "How do you know it doesn't fit?"
3. "I don't know — the color looks good to me."
4. "What do you mean, you don't want it?"

By continuing to answer questions with questions instead of answers you will guarantee yourself less future business.

And speaking of the future, from what base do you expect to achieve next year's increase? Demographics are changing.

There are more people in the U.S. over 55 than there are teen-agers.

By 1990 more than half the population will be over 55.

What this means: There's not a heck of a lot new customers coming in your front door unless your business is geriatric-related.

So if you expect an increase in tomorrow's business (all who do, raise your hands) well, you better start with today's customer.

Most retailers take their existing customer for granted. They ignore time-proven surveys revealing:

A. Nearly 70 percent of customers who leave your store do so for **no specific reason!**

B. A satisfied customer tells three other people about your store. A dissatisfied customer tells eleven other people about your store.

Dr. Russell Conwell said it best 100 years ago. In fact, he said it more than 6,000 times over a 50-year period in one basic speech called, "Acres of Diamonds." His theme : "There's vast unplotted areas of opportunity in your own backyard." (See chapter # 14, "Acres of Diamonds.")

It worked for Conwell — this one speech netted him millions of dollars — much of which he used to found Temple University.

What does his speech have to do with you as a retailer?

This: Inside of every old customer you have is a new customer waiting to break out and spend more money with you.

Most retailers find this hard to believe. "Why, Sara Rosen just spent a few hundred dollars on clothes with me. She can't afford to buy any more. . ."

Really? What does she have in the giant shopping bag she just brought home from your competitor?

"An often neglected method of achieving sales is the existing customer. It is easier to expand from an already loyal base then to convert non-shoppers to shoppers." So says Paul Le Blang. He should know. As Saks Fifth Avenue's vice president and director of marketing, he achieves consistent and ongoing increases with his quality direct mail, much of which is directed to his existing customer base.

Bonwit Teller agrees. They pinpoint three major groups: women executives, wives of top male executives and younger customers in middle management. They want to build business with their own customers who are building their businesses. Their theory: Take care of the customer and the customer takes care of you.

Bloomingdale's agrees. They put out a furniture catalog to customers who buy their furniture. Sales increased 40 percent!

The success stories of retailers who increase their business with **customers they have with the most effective medium they have — direct mail — fills hundreds of pages this size.**

It all begins by answering your customer's question **not with a question but with an answer!**

So the next time your customer says:
1. "I have problem. . ."
2. "I'm dissatisfied with you. . ."
3. "What are you going to do about. . ."
You answer to **all the above** is, "I'm here to take care of you. When you walk out the front door, you will be satisfied. That's **my answer** to your question."

37

Six Common Characteristics of Successful Business People.

I have an understanding with my doctor. I agree not to tell him how to run his medical operation if he agrees not to tell me how to run my retail operation.

We live in an age of instant. Instant coffee. Instant soup. Instant communication. And instant knowledge. Everyone feels that he or she is an expert in decision-making or reason-finding whenever a business goes bankrupt, a government falls or the Dallas Cowboys lose.

Monday-morning quarterbacks and kibitzers in card games are both accepted. Each begins his theory with the same statements, "If only they had. . ." or "The way I would have done it was. . ."

I have a theory on all this. It works like this: If my business is good, it's because I am good. It's because I'm smart and I know what the customer wants to buy. It's because I watch my business and when sales are off I come up with a new idea, a new mailing, a new way to communicate with the customer I have.

And if my business is bad. . .

It's not the weather. It's not the economy. It's not the time of the year. It's me. **I'm doing something wrong.**

People are spending money somewhere. My job: Find out how to have them spend that money with me.

In order to do that, I need a plan. A goal. A specific target to aim at. If my customer is a specific person (and they are!) then my goal must be just as specific.

First of all, I start off with confidence in myself and my merchandise. I cannot inspire an acceptance from others unless I have a personal belief.

What do you think of **yourself**?

What do you think of **your** business?

What goals have you set for yourself for next month? Next year? Five years from now?

Unless you have a specific plan for your business, you cannot succeed. Would you travel on a plane with a pilot who did not know where he was flying? Or a captain who had no idea where the ship was going?

A recent article in *The Wall Street Journal* said a prominent psychologist narrowed down the difference between performers and non-performers to six characteristics.

"Today, millionaires are a dime a dozen" said a San Jose State University psychology professor, "We're looking for those who go beyond that."

Here are the six characteristics.

How many describe you?

How many describe your business?

1. They constantly set higher goals.

They are mountain climbers who, having climbed one peak, look beyond to the next peak. They are proud of the fact that of 10,000 mailers sent to their customers, nearly 1,000 came to the store for the sale. Now, the question is, how can they increase that number to 1,500 the next time around.

2. They avoid "comfort zones."

They know standing still means going backwards. They know most other retailers work on the "lawnmower" theory. They do things the way they were always done in the past because it is "comfortable." Others follow the same pattern, work the same techniques, avoid the new, the different, the unusual on the fear they might do something wrong. Their mailing piece looks the same every year, because once, a dozen mailers ago, the original was very successful. The lack of continuing success they blame on the weather, the time of the year, the new competition, anything except themselves.

3. Their drives are accomplishments not money.

They follow the theory of Steve Job of Apple (and his new "Next") computer fame who says, "The journey is the reward."

Their thrill is not the ringing of the register but the crowds responding to the mailing. There is no greater "high" than the making-of-the-sale, the bringing-of-the-crowd, the line outside the store before the door is open, because of what you did to bring them there.

4. They solve problems rather than place blame.

They will not waste their time wondering "What if. . ." or "Why didn't you. . . " They say, "Let's look at what went wrong and figure out how we can make it go right next time." They understand the importance of "testing" in their mailings and are quick to try the new, the different, the unusual and are flexible enough to adjust, maneuver, change direction to that-which-works. They know the road to success is constantly under repair. And they work at it.

5. They look at the worst possible scenario.

"What's the worst possible result if we follow this plan?," they ask themselves. Knowing that, they then decide if the risk-taking is practical.

However, once they decide to go ahead, they proceed with confidence, with the knowledge, the talent and the expertise they have to make-it-work.

They know the worst that can happen and decide if they can live with that outcome. If they can, they move ahead. Confidently.

We see this plan in action with companies that produce successful catalogs. They then decide to reach into other unrelated areas. Sometimes they succeed. Sometimes they do not. But they look at each defeat as a learning experience.

"Everytime I fail," said Thomas Edison, "I learn something." (He tried 1,114 times to find a filament to stay lit in a bulb. He failed 1,113 times.)

6. They rehearse the future as they see it.

The success people are telelogical. That means they move toward the pictures they create in their mind. They can rehearse coming actions or events as they "see" them. They are like chess players who can "feel" the next move of their opponent and have a half dozen responses ready to take when their time comes to move.

The Russians believe in the concept of studying why some individuals out perform others. They call this concept "anthropomaximology." What that means: Society is no longer satisfied with simply "success." They want to know the difference between the successful and the most successful.

Businesses go bankrupt in the United States every year. Who will be the successful business person who remains? The one who will be here when others have gone? The one who the customers will seek out to shop and spend with and say this is the place not only where they will spend their money but also where they recommend their friends come and spend as well?

How many of the six characteristics are yours? How many belong to your store? The more you have, the higher degree of probability you will be in the same old stand on the same old spot doing not the same but more business next year. Instead of being one of the 35,000 retailers who were listed in the business obituary pages last year.

38

The Invisible Horses

It was World War 11. An American general was doing an air surveillance of British artillery units. He noticed they would load their cannon, close the breech and then, suddenly, step back a few paces behind the cannons with their hand clenched away from their sides.

"Why are they doing that?" asked the general. No one knew. After lengthy investigation, they finally found an elderly English brigadier who explained, "Why they're simply 'olding the 'orses."

Holding the horses? Of course. In earlier days the artillery was horse-drawn. When the cannon was loaded, the artillery men took a few paces backwards just before they fired, and held the reins of the horses in their hands to keep them from running off.

The horses were replaced by trucks for many years, but the artillery men continued to "old the 'orses."

Remember the Reason For the Rules

Often, the problem with setting up rules to follow is there comes a time when someone forgets why the rules were set-up in the first place. And, the Hatfields and McCoys continue to fight the same battles when no one remembers the reason why.

Rules for direct mail work pretty much the same way. You are taught what should be done, and follow the learned phrases, techniques and concepts religiously. If someone steps forward and says, "Uh, I didn't do rule number two and I was successful," he or she is quickly reminded what my Latin teacher once told me: "That's the exception that proves the rule."

Really? Or should we constantly experiment, innovate, and even violate the accepted principles?

No. And then again, yes.

No when we're dealing with "givens" such as spelling the name right and using the name instead of "occupant," and enclosing a response card to have the reader become involved and. . . well, you get the idea.

Yes when we are willing to risk the new, the different, the unusual, just because it "feels" right to do it.

Here are some shibboleths you hear people repeat as gospel. And how the rules were broken, ignored, cast aside. . . and how success followed anyway.

1. You must have an order blank in your mail order ad. Because. . . how can customers order the merchandise without an order blank?

Suddenly, from the Midwest, Joe Sugarman rides into town with his JS&A mail order company that eliminates the order blank and substitutes an 800 number. "Why an order blank?" asked Joe. "Why not a telephone number, which means faster orders and faster response?"

Uh, Joe didn't you ever hear the story about the Invisible Horses?

2. You must tell your story quickly, upfront. Because. . . readers get bored. They won't wade through paragraphs of material trying to figure out what you want to sell them. So quick, fast, tell them at once what it's all about.

Not according to Bill Jayme's results-proven subscription letter for Science Magazine. He wrote the entire first page about an ancient way of telling time through the use of sunlight and rocks!

Not according to John Fraser-Robinson, who won a European award for his fund-raising letter for the St. John's ambulance society that talked about women swooning and an English goose for the first page and a half.

3. You must sell merchandise in season. Because. . . no one wants to buy swimsuits in winter or long underwear in June.

Not according to L.L. Bean, whose sales doubled and tripled when they switched from biannual (Spring/Summer, Fall/Winter) catalog mailings to monthly mailings that enabled customers to buy when **they** felt like it.

4. Use short copy. Because. . . everyone knows you have to follow the Keep It Short & Simple (K.I.S.S.) rules in direct mail. Direct mail seminars list the number of words customers will read before their attention lags. Quick. Fast. At once. Short. Abrupt. That's what people want.

Not according to Merrill Lynch which ran an ad in *The New York Times* with more than **10,000** words; and thousands of reader wrote for more information on the products and services.

Not according to Boyce Morgan, the writer responsible for many of the early direct mail successes of the Kiplinger Letter. He conducted tests on long vs. short copy. His results: When you cut copy down to fit on one sheet of paper, you also cut down on orders.

5. Expensive merchandise needs an expensive setting. Because . . . you should make the copy and layout "fit," according to one of the seven principles laid down years ago by Ed Mayer. As Ed said: You don't go swimming in a tuxedo, and you don't go to a fancy dinner in a bathing suit. If you sell expensive merchandise, the mailer must look expensive.

Not according to art salesman Reese Palley. He bought lithographs of the four face cards (Jack, Queen, King and Ace) from Salvador Dali, and offered them to his customers for $650 apiece. The received a free trip for the weekend to Paris on a 747 if they bought one.

Reese sold out **two** 747's to his mailing list of a few thousand with a simple black and white mailer that cost him about five cents each. His return was somewhere in the millions of dollars!

Now, this is **NOT** a cry to tear up the rule books and plunge into uncharted waters. You must know **what** you are doing and **why** you are doing it. It was my Latin teacher (again) who said, "You can break any rule you want, as long as you know what the rule is and why you are breaking it."

And so this is a call for non-traditional thinking. To examine what you are doing with a fresh look, an unjaundiced eye, a willingness to experiment. For while it is true that fools rush in where angels fear to tread, it is also true that he who hesitates is lost.

Years ago, in Russia, a Czar came upon a lonely sentry standing at attention in a secluded corner of the palace gardens.

"What are you guarding?" asked the Czar.

"I don't know. The captain ordered me to this post," the sentry replied.

The Czar called the captain for an explanation. His answer: Written regulations specified a guard was to be assigned to that area.

The Czar ordered a search to find out why. The archives finally yielded the reason. Years before, Catherine the Great had planted a rose bush in that corner of the garden. She ordered a Sentry to protect it for that evening.

One hundred years later, sentries were still guarding the now barren spot. . .

39

The Quest To Be Best.

It was a cold overcast rainy day in Iffley, London. The morning chill mist hung over the running track at Oxford University. The day: May 7, 1954.

Roger Bannister was going to try to run the mile in less than four minutes.

"Impossible," said the experts.

"Can't be done," echoed the sportscasters.

"The human heart cannot handle the strain," opined the medical man.

Some records of stamina and endurance cannot be broken simply because of the limitations of the human body, explained those in the know.

Bannister knew this was the accepted line of reason. He also knew scientists could prove the weight of a bee's body was out of proportion to the size of his wings. Aerodynamically, the bee cannot fly. But the bee does not know this. And so he flies...

The race begins! Brasher goes into the lead followed by Bannister and then Chataway. Near the half mile Chataway takes the lead with Bannister following.

In the last 250 yards Bannister sprints to the front, breaks the tape and because the first human to run a mile in under four minutes.

In the next few months, this record was broken repeatedly. In the next few years, hundreds of runners ran the mile in less than four minutes. An impossible achievement made possible because one man said he would set out — and achieve — his personal. . . Quest to be Best.

* * *

Most businesses reflect the thinking of the doubters, the skeptics, those that say "Why bother?" or "The risk is too great," or, simply, "It can't be done."

Yet most businesses are capable of operating, and succeeding, at much higher levels.

Most businesses do not strive for excellence simply because it is far easier, less complicated and no challenge to continue just-as-you-are.

"How much more business do you plan to do next year?" we asked a fellow retailer.

"Oh, a 10 percent increase would be fine," he said.

"How about a 100 percent increase?" we asked, "doubling your business?"

"A 100 percent increase?" he asked in disbelief.

"Yes," we said, "what would you have to do to achieve that goal?"

He thought for a moment and then said, "Well, let's see. I'd have to tear out that wall, make more room for stock, increase my advertising, work with my salespeople in new areas. . ."

As he continued we realized he had originally set his increase at 10 percent because it was comfortable, attainable, no problem.

A larger increase meant new ways of working, new challenges, new risks. . . a quest to be good, better. . . best.

What would happen to our retailing friend if, in fact, he set a goal to double his business and only attained a **40 percent increase?**

When he would have settled for only . . . 10 percent.

Most retailers are content to settle for mediocrity.

We mailed a letter to 40 menswear stores across the U.S.

inviting them to join us for a buying trip at the annual Scandinavian Fashion Fair in Stockholm. They would find merchandise they could have exclusive in their trading areas from European manufacturers. We told of our success with these lines and a special air fare/hotel package. No one answered, so we called several to ask "Why?" The answers ranged from "Well, we never did that before" to "I can't take the time" to other nonsensical replies. That was three years ago. Are many of the 40 now out of business just because of their failure to go on this trip? No. Are many out of business because of their failure to accept that which was new, different and challenging? Yes!

They are content to get along and go along in the same rutted and familiar paths that create no extra work.

What has happened? This: Work has become work and not fun. It is a time to seriously think about doing something else instead.

Once you set a personal, seemingly unattainable goal, once you are no longer satisfied with what is but yearn instead for what-might-be, once you reach over, above and beyond, then you have begun your own, personal and individual "Quest to be Best."

We talk a lot about direct mail for the small business throughout this book. Here's why: Direct mail is a personal communication between you and your customer. Line extension from one-on-one relationship in the business to one-on-one relationship through the mail box.

This special offer for this special customer means extra special results. If you haven't tried direct mail — you should. Always be ready to try something new. Something different (and, in this case something that works!)

What all this means: you have to constantly set goals to be the best. In fact you can actually "see" yourself winning: crossing the goal, closing the sale, winning the race.

Important: Do not confuse this setting of goals with making of money.

Those whose goals are to make money fail.

Those whose goals are to be the best in their field succeed.

"Money," said a successful Wall Street investor, "isn't why I do what I do. It's just a way of keeping score."

The most powerful indicators of individual rewards are not money but a quality of life. A Quest to be Best.

The way to achieve success in your business, and in your life is to first acknowledge you will settle for nothing but the best. And once do that, you have established the ground rule to guide you in the future.

In Japan, there is a rock garden between Tofuku-Ji, the tallest and most sacred Shinto shrine in the country, and the Ryoan-Ji temple. It is said this is the most perfect stone garden in existence and is exactly the same today as it was in the 15th century.

When you visit you will see an old man stooped over a long handle rake, carefully cleaning and resetting each pebble in the stone garden. Every stone has a meaning — the way they are arranged, the way they are placed, the location of the larger rocks. The achievement exists because of the planning that precedes. Because the original goal was simply, A Quest to be Best.